Faith in Mind

任運自在

雲嚴

FAITH
IN
MIND

A Guide to
Ch'an Practice

Master Sheng-yen

Acknowledgments

Editor	Karen Zinn
Editorial Assistance	Ernest Heau Richard Kent Alan Rubinstein
Translator (poem):	Master Sheng-yen
Co-Translator (poem):	Paul Kennedy
Interpreter: (retreat lectures)	Dan Stevenson Ming-Yee Wang Karen Zinn
Transcriber:	Dorothy Weiner
Book Design	Trish Ing Page Simon
Calligraphy	Master Sheng-yen
Illustration	Cliff Selover
Cover Design and Photography	Page Simon

Dharma Drum Publications is the publishing activity of

Institute of Chung-Hwa Buddhist Culture
90-56 Corona Avenue
Elmhurst, New York 11373

Library of Congress Catalog Card Number 70292
ISBN 0-9609854-2-5

Table of Contents

RETREAT FOUR

FAITH
IN
MIND

INTRODUCTION

In the records of Ch'an masters, there is no full account of the life of Seng Ts'an, the Third Patriarch, who died in A.D. 606. He is mentioned, however, in the T'ang dynasty (618-907) Kao Seng Chua *(Biographies of Eminent Monks)* written by master Fa Ts'ung; "After Ch'an master (Hui) K'o, there was Ch'an master (Seng) Ts'an." The Leng Ch'ieh Shih Tzu Chi *(Records of the Masters of the Lankavatara Sutra)*, which contains early historical material of the Ch'an school, says that after entering retreat in the mountains Seng Ts'an never emerged, nor did he ever write about or transmit the Dharma. This statement is problematic considering that the Sui dynasty history in Er Shih Wu Shih *(The Twenty-five History Books)* states that in 592 he transmitted the Dharma to Tao Hsin (580-651), the Fourth Patriarch. It also calls into question the authorship of the poem *Faith in Mind*, which has historically been attributed to Seng Ts'an. Contemporary scholars doubt whether he was, in fact, the author. Niu T'ou Fa Jung (594-657), a disciple of Tao Hsin, wrote a poem entitled *Song of Mind.* Noticing the similarity between the two poems, some suggest that *Faith in Mind* was actually written after the time of the Sixth Patriarch, Hui Neng (638-713), as an improved, condensed version of *Song of*

Mind. The thought expressed in *Faith in Mind* is indeed better organized, more concise and seems complete compared to Niu T'ou's poem.

The question of attribution, however, has no relevance to my commentaries on *Faith in Mind*. The importance of the poem to us lies in its value as a guide to Ch'an meditation, and its significance in the history of Ch'an (Zen), both in China and Japan. Among the many poems on enlightenment, the most highly regarded are Yung Chia's (665-713) *Song of Enlightenment,* and *Faith in Mind,* because of the clear guidance they provide on the method of Ch'an.

For this reason, I do not comment on *Faith in Mind* on ordinary occasions. I choose to lecture on it only during the seven-day Ch'an retreat. The twenty chapters of this book are based on translated lectures spanning four retreats, subsequently edited for publication. Since the talks were given within the context of intensive meditation practice, I did not adopt a scholarly point of view or analytical approach. It is not a formal commentary on the text; rather, I use the poem as a taking-off point to inspire the practitioner and deal with certain issues that arise during the course of practice.

There are at least five published English translations of *Faith in Mind.* All have their merits. I offer a new translation which is similar in many respects to previous ones; however, portions of it are quite different, reflecting my own understanding of the poem.

When commenting on *Faith in Mind*, I often say to my students, "Now that you are practicing, it matters little whether or not I speak on *Faith in Mind*. But I am using the poem to instruct you on the method of practice." The progress and condition of a given group of practitioners differs from day to day and from retreat to retreat. Thus I adapt my discussion of the poem to the situation at hand, while remaining within the scope of the text. I believe these talks can serve as a helpful guide both to the aspiring and experienced practitioner. It has also helped me personally, by giving me new insights into the poem as various situations arose.

The phrase "faith in mind" contains the two meanings of "believing in" and "realizing" the mind. "Mind" is especially emphasized in Ch'an. True faith in mind is the belief grounded in realization that we have a fundamental, unmoving, unchanging mind. This mind is precisely Buddha mind; it is also *Tathagatagarbha* (womb of Tathagata) in every sentient being. But the mind experienced by ordinary beings in the midst of vexations is deluded mind, not true mind. Those who seek to rid themselves of vexations imagine that there is a true mind to attain. However, from the perspective of Buddha mind, there is only one mind, neither true nor false. There is no need to discriminate, for everything, everywhere, is mind everlasting. When we fully realize Buddha mind, the believing mind and the mind which is believed in merge into one; since they are the same, the need for mere belief in this mind disappears.

The paradox is that one must be enlightened to have true faith in this mind. The author is speaking from a deeply enlightened perspective to the practitioner who

seeks to discover true mind. Seng Ts'an shows us how
to transform our ordinary discriminating mind into the
Buddha mind which does not discriminates; how to get
from existence to emptiness, from defilement to purity.
He tells us how we should practice and what kind of
mental attitude to avoid during practice: we should not
give in to our likes and dislikes, neither trying to negate
our vexations nor seeking enlightenment. The practice
should be pursued for its own sake, but while there
should be no other purpose, in the end the mind of equanimity *(ping deng hsin)* is realized — there is no discrimination, no need for language *(yen yu tao tuan)*, or, indeed, of practice.

The poem contains phrases that will later on assume
importance in the Ts'ao Tung (Soto) sect of Ch'an, for
instance, "One thought for ten thousand years" *(i nien
wan nien)*, which expresses the idea of one thought not
moving and yet illuminating. This idea is to become the
hallmark of Hung Chih Cheng Chueh's Silent Illumination Ch'an. This tendency is also repeated in the only
other written record of Seng Ts'an's teachings which was
found on a stone tablet commemorating him. The essence
of the inscription is: Simultaneously practice stillness *(chi)*
and illumination *(chao)*. Carefully observe, but see no
dharmas (phenomena), see no body, and see no mind. For
the mind is nameless, the body is empty, and the dharmas
are a dream. There is nothing to be attained, no enlightenment to be experienced. This is called liberation.

Faith In Mind

The Supreme Way is not difficult
If only you do not pick and choose.
Neither love nor hate,
And you will clearly understand.
Be off by a hair,
And you are as far from it as heaven from earth.
If you want the Way to appear,
Be neither for nor against.
For and against opposing each other —
This is the mind's disease.
Without recognizing the mysterious principle
It is useless to practice quietude.
The Way is perfect like great space,
Without lack, without excess.
Because of grasping and rejecting,
You cannot attain it.
Do not pursue conditioned existence;
Do not abide in acceptance of emptiness.
In oneness and equality,
Confusion vanishes of itself.
Stop activity and return to stillness,
And that stillness will be even more active.

Merely stagnating in duality,
How can you recognize oneness?
If you fail to penetrate oneness,
Both places lose their function.
Banish existence and you fall into existence;
Follow emptiness and you turn your back on it.
Excessive talking and thinking
Turn you from harmony with the Way.
Cut off talking and thinking,
And there is nowhere you cannot penetrate.
Return to the root and attain the principle;
Pursue illumination and you lose it.
One moment of reversing the light
Is greater than the previous emptiness.
The previous emptiness is transformed;
It was all a product of deluded views.
No need to seek the real;
Just extinguish your views.
Do not abide in dualistic views;
Take care not to seek after them.
As soon as there is right and wrong
The mind is scattered and lost.
Two comes from one,
Yet do not even keep the one.
When one mind does not arise,
Myriad dharmas are without defect.

Without defect, without dharmas,
No arising, no mind.
The subject is extinguished with the object.
The object sinks away with the subject.
Object is object because of the subject;
Subject is subject because of the object.
Know that the two
Are originally one emptiness.
In one emptiness the two are the same,
Containing all phenomena.
Not seeing fine or coarse,
How can there be any bias?
The Great Way is broad,
Neither easy nor difficult.
With narrow views and doubts,
Haste will slow you down.
Attach to it and you lose the measure;
The mind will enter a deviant path.
Let it go and be spontaneous,
Experience no going or staying.
Accord with your nature, unite with the Way,
Wander at ease, without vexation.
Bound by thoughts, you depart from the real;
And sinking into a stupor is as bad.
It is not good to weary the spirit.
Why alternate between aversion and affection?

If you wish to enter the one vehicle,
Do not be repelled by the sense realm.
With no aversion to the sense realm,
You become one with true enlightenment.
The wise have no motives;
Fools put themselves in bondage.
One dharma is not different from another.
The deluded mind clings to whatever it desires.
Using mind to cultivate mind —
Is this not a great mistake?
The erring mind begets tranquillity and confusion;
In enlightenment there are no likes or dislikes.
The duality of all things
Issues from false discriminations.
A dream, an illusion, a flower in the sky —
How could they be worth grasping?
Gain and loss, right and wrong —
Discard them all at once.
If the eyes do not close in sleep,
All dreams will cease of themselves.
If the mind does not discriminate,
All dharmas are of one suchness.
The essence of one suchness is profound;
Unmoving, conditioned things are forgotten.
Contemplate all dharmas as equal,
And you return to things as they are.

When the subject disappears,
There can be no measuring or comparing.
Stop activity and there is no activity;
When activity stops, there is no rest.
Since two cannot be established,
How can there be one?
In the very ultimate,
Rules and standards do not exist.
Develop a mind of equanimity,
And all deeds are put to rest.
Anxious doubts are completely cleared.
Right faith is made upright.
Nothing lingers behind,
Nothing can be remembered.
Bright and empty, functioning naturally,
The mind does not exert itself.
It is not a place of thinking,
Difficult for reason and emotion to fathom.
In the Dharma Realm of true suchness,
There is no other, no self.
To accord with it is vitally important;
Only refer to "not-two."
In not-two all things are in unity;
Nothing is excluded.
The wise throughout the ten directions
All enter this principle.

This principle is neither hurried nor slow —
One thought for ten thousand years.
Abiding nowhere yet everywhere,
The ten directions are right before you.
The smallest is the same as the largest
In the realm where delusion is cut off.
The largest is the same as the smallest;
No boundaries are visible.
Existence is precisely emptiness;
Emptiness is precisely existence.
If it is not like this,
Then you must not preserve it.
One is everything;
Everything is one.
If you can be like this,
Why worry about not finishing?
Faith and mind are not two;
Non-duality is faith in mind.
The path of words is cut off;
There is no past, no future, no present.

Retreat One

November 23, 1984 – November 30, 1984

1
Embarking on the Practice

The Supreme Way is not difficult
If only you do not pick and choose.
Neither love nor hate,
And you will clearly understand.
Be off by a hair,
And you are as far from it as heaven from earth.

The sole purpose of a Ch'an retreat is to meditate. You should keep your attention entirely on practice, without trying to attain any results. Since many of you have traveled far, or have worked hard to set aside the time, you have a great deal invested in this retreat. It is natural that you want to gain something. But once you enter the retreat, you must put aside any specific hopes.

Practicing with a goal in mind is like trying to catch a feather with a fan. The more you go after it, the more it eludes you. But if you sneak up on it slowly, you can grab it. The aim of practice is to develop patience and forbearance, to train your mind to become calm and stable. Any attachment or seeking will prevent your mind from settling down.

Today someone told me that the more he worked on the *hua-t'ou*[1] the more tense he felt. It was as though his mind had become knotted up. His problem is that he wants to see quick results. Pursuing the *hua-t'ou* intensely with a desire to get enlightened is like tying yourself up and then poking yourself with a knife. The more you drive yourself the more tense you will feel. The same principle applies to the body. If you react to pain by tensing the body, the pain will only get worse. If any part of your body feels painful, you should try to relax it. Any involuntary movement of the body while sitting in meditation is also due to tension. Thus it is important to constantly maintain a state of relaxation.

Related to this are the problems that may develop from fixing your attention on a particular part of the body. For instance, some people try to make their breath flow smoothly. But in trying to control the breath, it becomes abnormal.

Don't pay attention to any phenomenon that occurs to the body; if you are concerned with it, problems will arise. It is the same with the mind. You will be unable to practice unless you disregard everything that happens to you mentally. If you feel distressed or pained in any way, just ignore it. Let it go and return wholeheartedly to the method. Place your mind directly on the method itself; concern yourself with nothing else.

The Supreme Way in the first line of the poem refers to the stage of Buddhahood. The wisdom of the Buddha is not difficult to perceive; it can be attained in the instant between two thoughts. The reason for this is that it has never been separate from us. It is always present. In fact, we all desire to realize this Supreme Way. If so, why are we unable to attain it?

The second line explains what prevents us. It is because we are always trying to escape our vexations. Precisely because we want to acquire the Buddha's insight and merits, we are unable to perceive Buddha nature.

Another reason why we cannot see our Buddha nature is that we are burdened with ideas. We make distinctions between *samsara*[2] and *nirvana*[3], sentient beings and the Buddha, vexations and enlightenment. These ideas obstruct our perception of Buddha nature.

To paraphrase lines three and four: As soon as you discard your likes and dislikes, the Way will immediately appear before you. Here, Seng-Ts'an has something in common with Tao-Hsin, the Fourth Patriarch, and Hui-Neng, the Sixth Patriarch. The latter two frequently said that when you stop discriminating between good and evil, you will immediately perceive your "original face." (In Ch'an "original face" refers to one's innate Buddha nature.) In other words, you will understand the Supreme Way.

When sitting, some of you are distracted with pain, or are trying to fight off drowsiness. At night, maybe you are angry at someone who is keeping you awake with his snoring. But instead of letting it annoy you, just observe the snoring. Soon the snores may become hypnotic and repetitive, actually pleasant sounding. If you start counting the snores, before you know it you will be asleep.

On the other hand, becoming attached to a certain

pleasurable experience in meditation can also be an obstruction. One student I had would rock her body during sitting meditation. She felt that she had no control over the shaking; it just happened spontaneously. Actually, this was not caused by any physical tension but by a subconscious motive. The rocking was comfortable to her. You cannot practice effectively if you give in to such things. By examining them, you will be able to control the mind.

Holding on to various likes and dislikes keeps you apart from the Way. Discarding them will bring you in accord with the Way. But if there is the slightest misconception about this, the distance between you and the Way will be as great as that between heaven and earth. Don't misinterpret this and think that since you are not supposed to attach to likes and dislikes, you should therefore not cultivate the Way. With this attitude it is useless to come on a Ch'an retreat.

When you first set out to practice you will definitely have a goal in mind. You may be frustrated with your present condition and aim either to change yourself or to improve your circumstances. Certainly there is something you hope to achieve by practicing. You cannot just practice aimlessly. So practice itself implies some intention or desire. To fulfill your original intentions, you must constantly keep your mind on the method of practice. But as you focus on the method you should not be thinking of what you want to accomplish, what level you want to reach, or what problems you want to get rid of. Instead, your mind should be exclusively applied to the method itself, free from all other motives.

There is a saying that is useful for practitioners: "Put down the myriad thoughts. Take up the practice." The myriad thoughts are scattered, random, extraneous concerns. The practice is your method of cultivation. When your mind wanders to extraneous concerns, put them down as soon as they appear. But should you treat the method in the same way as a wandering thought — putting it down as soon as it appears? No. From moment to moment, put down extraneous thoughts and return your mind to the method of practice.

One time I asked a student, "Are you having many extraneous thoughts?" He replied, "Not too many." I said, "I'll bet I know one of them. You're thinking of your girl friend all the time, aren't you?" He retorted, "How can you say that?" After the retreat he said, "Originally, I wasn't thinking of my girl friend at all. But after *Shih-fu*[4] mentioned her I couldn't stop thinking of her." I told him that he hadn't seen through his problem yet. He may have thought that his mind was not on his girl friend, but his concern was still there.

Perhaps you try to put down extraneous concerns but find that you just can't. Every time you put one down, it comes back again. This upsets you. You keep telling yourself, "Put it down. Put it down." Actually it doesn't matter if you can't put it down. If you eventually get to the point where you say to yourself, "It doesn't matter if I can't put it down," then you will be putting it down. You should not fear failure. Neither should you embrace it. You may conclude that the retreat is just not going well for you — your body is uncomfortable, your mind is in tumult. You are unable to control yourself. You haven't made the proper preparations. So you think, why not forget this one and leave tomorrow? Maybe I'll try again the next time. But don't succumb to this defeatist attitude. A Chinese proverb says: "A hundred birds in a tree are not worth one bird in the palm." If you let go of that one bird to go after the hundred you will end up with nothing. Even though you feel unprepared and doomed to failure, being here still presents a wonderful opportunity to practice.

(1) *hua-t'ou:* (Japanese: *wato*). Literally, "the source of the words," a method used in the Ch'an school to arouse the great doubt sensation to induce the mind to break through to the enlightened state. The practitioner meditates on such baffling questions as: "What is *wu*?" "Where am I?" or "Who is reciting Buddha's name?" Often, the phrase is taken from a *kung-an* (Japanese: *koan*).

(2) *samsara:* (Sanskrit, "journeying"). The cycle of birth and death experienced by all sentient beings; the phenomenal world in which the cycle takes place. Liberation from the samsaric cycle results in entering the state of *nirvana*.

(3) *nirvana:* (Sanskrit, "extinction"). In Buddhism, the goal of spiritual practice is to liberate oneself from *samsara*, the cycle of birth and death, and to enter the state of unconditioned existence, *nirvana*.

(4) *Shih-fu:* ("teacher-father"). A term of respect used by a disciple when referring to or addressing his master.

2
Overcoming Like and Dislike

If you want the Way to appear,
Be neither for nor against.
For and against opposing each other —
This is the mind's disease.

If you want the Buddha Way to manifest before your eyes, it is a mistake to harbor any preferences or aversions. This includes anything you hope to acquire, keep, discard, or avoid. When sitting seems to be going particularly well, the idea may pop into your mind that you are about to be enlightened. You begin to wait for this enlightenment experience. With this expectation, the mind has already abandoned its single-mindedness and has become confused and scattered. You will not be able to maintain your previous state of concentration. On a prior retreat, one student was progressing so well that there were notable changes in his mental state. At that point he became frightened. He thought, "I'm happy with the way I am now. I don't really want any drastic changes. What if my friends don't recognize me?" He did not sit as well for the rest of the retreat.

This contradictory mentality often afflicts the practitioner. He wants to enter the door of enlightenment but at the same time is really afraid of entering. You come to a retreat with the desire to transform yourself. Indeed, practice can make you more mature, calm, and stable. It will certainly not change you into something less human, or ghostlike. Since ancient times all of the numerous practitioners who have gotten deeply enlightened remained human, the only difference being that afterward they were more stable and filled with wisdom. There is no reason to fear changing that way.

Such a contradictory state of mind is common among ordinary people. When I left home as a young boy I was very excited about becoming a monk. But on the other hand, I had never been to a monastery and had some apprehension. I just did not know what would happen there. Many people who believe in heaven have similar fears about what it will be like after death.

These contradictions point to inherent weaknesses in our personality, of which we are usually unaware. It is only in the context of practice that these weaknesses are exposed. Once we discover and understand our weaknesses, we can prevent them from further obstructing our practice.

Though "for" and "against" are opposites, they are also very much related. If there is something that you like, there must be something else that you dislike. And if you cannot get what you like, you will change your mind and dislike it. To be caught in this conflict between like and dislike is a serious disease of the mind. It is a barrier to practice. Practice is a process by which we recognize and treat the disease of our minds. When the disease completely disappears, the ultimate Way is revealed.

Without recognizing the mysterious principle
It is useless to practice quietude.

If you do not grasp the deep truth in the previous lines, no matter how hard you practice, your efforts will be futile. This is because there is a struggle within your mind. The previous thought is continually at war with the following thought. Under these circumstances, it is almost impossible to attain a peaceful state of mind.

Even if you do manage to overcome your scattered thoughts and reach a peaceful state, it would still be useless. You will be so happy to have entered this state that you will grasp it and not let it go. In the end, you will not have achieved a concentrated mind but an attached mind. Nonetheless, a peaceful state of mind is at least better than one involved in a constant internal struggle. As long as you live alone you may be able to maintain it. But if you have to interact with people, things may start bothering you. You may be disturbed by the noise of children, visits of friends or stress at work. Eventually, you will seek to avoid these things and meditate alone in a room.

Someone here has a habit of sometimes falling backwards while sitting. Today I cautioned her that if she does it hard enough, the shock may cause her to lose consciousness or even her ability to think rationally. She remarked, "That's not such a bad idea, after all. Now I have to struggle with all of the problems in my mind. If I get such a shock, my problems will simply disappear." I said, "That may be the case, but who will feed you and take care of you? Who will take care of your children?" A shock to your nervous system is not the same as enlightenment. Rather, it is a disease. Just because a person does not have any scattered thoughts does not mean that all his problems are resolved. If all you are interested in is a thoughtless state, just ask someone to hit you hard on the back of your head. There are too many people who cannot distinguish between true wisdom and a mere state of peacefulness. If you do not understand this distinction, even if you practice hard, at best you are being foolish.

You should not remain passively in peacefulness. Don't be afraid of difficulties. If your mind cannot settle down you should not feel any resentment. Cultivate non-aversion to the unpleasant and non-attachment to the pleasant. Taking a pleasurable state for enlightenment will get you into trouble. Enlightenment is not something we have to guard fiercely, not letting it go. If a pleasant state arises, don't get stuck on it, just continue to practice.

On a past retreat one person sat through four thirty-minute periods without stirring. Seeing that his condition was "too good," I struck him with the incense board.[1] Thereupon he grabbed the board and hit me, saying, "I was in such a blissful state and now I have lost *samadhi*."[2] Aside from the fact that practitioners should not have any attachments, it is not the purpose of Ch'an to remain in samadhi. It is not necessarily good for the mind to settle down too quickly. Ch'an is a lively practice. It is not difficult to maintain a calm mind in a stationary situation. But in Ch'an one should be able to retain mental calmness even in a mobile state.

> *The Way is perfect like great space,*
> *Without lack, without excess.*
> *Because of grasping and rejecting,*
> *You cannot attain it.*

Great space does not refer to a nothingness, but rather to a totality. Though it includes everything, there is no individual existence. There is only the total, universal existence. Even before attaining the Way, practitioners should train themselves in the proper attitudes of one who is already enlightened. That is, they should discard the mentality of liking and disliking. So long as you practice diligently, that practice is the totality. After all, what you dislike and what you like are not separate from one another.

There was a landowner who hired many helping hands to work his fields. They were very good workers, but they had large appetites. On the one hand, he was pleased with their work but, on the other, he was annoyed that they ate so much. In the owner's mind this was a grave defect. To him it would be ideal if they would just do their job and not have to eat. Thus there is no need to rejoice when you think you have gotten what you like — it will bring with it things you dislike, and vice versa.

For example, a couple may spend a lot of time and energy courting each other. Eventually they are married and are very happy together. But along with the happiness there are also some restrictions. They feel stuck in the daily routine and lack the freedom to do whatever they want. They reflect that there is a certain merit to remaining single. But at this point, it is already too late.

When we think we have gotten something, we have not really gotten it and when we think we have lost something, we have not really lost it. This is because in the reality of totality, there is no gain and no loss. There is nothing outside of your mind. It is because you choose and reject that you are not free. It is for this reason that you have an excess or a lack. You have an excess of what you want to be rid of, and a lack of what you want to acquire. It is only when there is no grasping or rejecting that there will be neither excess nor lack.

(1) incense board: (Chinese: *hsiang-pan;* Japanese: *kyosaku*) A long, flat board used in the meditation hall to hit dozing practitioners or to help provide the final impetus to realization for those who are "ripe."

(2) *samadhi:* Refers to states of meditative absorption characterized by an expanded sense of self, or "one mind." The meditator loses normal awareness of body and surroundings.

3
Letting Go of Attachments

Do not pursue conditioned existence;
Do not abide in acceptance of emptiness.

People can be attached either to existence, the outer world, or emptiness, the inner void. Most of us are probably attached to existence, clinging to our thoughts, our body, the environment around us. On the other hand, someone attached to emptiness may think: "Since there is nothing after death, it is the simplest solution for everything. After I die, I won't have to worry about anything anymore." Another emptiness attitude may be: "Since the world is illusory, then nothing matters and I can stay detached from everything." Those who are attached to emptiness may have a devil-may-care attitude. They may refuse to take anything in life seriously. Or they may even be susceptible to committing suicide.

Attachment to either existence or to emptiness are improper attitudes. I have spoken of the dangers of attaching to existence — grasping what you like and rejecting what you dislike. But to say that there is nothing to grasp and nothing to reject is also incorrect — this would be attaching to emptiness. A person may be meditating with

a blank mind, apparently free of all thoughts and concerns. While this may seem to be approaching enlightenment, it is actually quite different. In the enlightened state,
a previous thought did not arise, a future thought will not
arise, and a present thought does not arise. But someone
in the blank state is just sitting there not thinking about or
doing anything. In fact, he is not practicing. Indeed he
does have a thought, which is: the previous thought arose,
but it does not matter. A future thought may arise but,
again, it does not matter. As to the present thought, let it
be. This person may think that he has no attachment to his
thoughts. But actually this is far from a true state of enlightenment. This kind of state is called "stubborn emptiness," as opposed to true emptiness, which is a lively state
of mind, full of awareness.

If you practice to a point where you feel very tranquil,
stable, and comfortable, that would be a peaceful state of
mind. The best you can attain in this peaceful condition is
a high samadhi state in the formless realm called the "emptiness samadhi." But if you become attached to such a
state you would never see your self- nature. This would be
considered an "outer path" practice.

In oneness and equality,
Confusion vanishes of itself.

Perceiving that all is one means making no distinction
between sage and sentient being, or between subject and
object. This is another way of describing the totality of
space. When you experience everything as equal, all distinctions will naturally disappear. While remembering not

to abide either in existence or emptiness, you should also know that existence and emptiness are not separate.

Yet is everything really the same? Once I said that the Buddha sees all sentient beings as the same, and is aware of every single thought in the universe. Someone raised the point that if the Buddha's mind was constantly being bombarded with such a tremendous influx of thoughts, it would not be a very comfortable state. This would mean that the Buddha's mind is like a garbage can and the thoughts of all sentient beings are being dumped into it. It would be a heavy burden on the Buddha.

If you take a snapshot with a high quality camera, everything in front of the lens will be imprinted on the film in minute detail. You can see the tip of each blade of grass and the outline of every leaf. Yet the camera does not think: "How annoying! All this junk is trying to get my attention." No. In one shot, it takes in everything without making distinctions among the objects — whether they are good or bad, long or short, green or yellow. But just because the camera does not make distinctions does not mean that the images on the film will appear confused or in the wrong order. On the contrary, everything is there clearly, and in place.

The Buddha's mind is like this. Having an equal mind means that there is no conception of relativity between things. Everything is absolute in the sense that there is no separation between you and others, between past and future. Because you see everything as equal, you would not choose one thing over another. Yet as soon as there are no longer any differences, it is as if existence simply disappears. For example, if everybody were male, the label "men" would no longer be meaningful, since its only purpose is to distinguish men from women. Everyone being the same, there would be no need for names. If you take an equal attitude towards everything, all differences will disappear, along with existence itself.

Once I handed the incense board to a student and asked him, "What is this?" He grabbed the board and shook it a few times. He did that because there was no name for it. We may call it an incense board but this is only our mind making distinctions. Why must we call it "incense board"?

During a retreat, I stood in front of a certain person. I asked him, "Who is standing in front of you?" He replied, "An egg." I was very pleased to be an egg.

When the retreat was over, I asked him, "Why is Shih-fu an egg?" He answered, "When Shih-fu asked me the question I did not have any thought whatsoever in my mind. Since I had to give an answer, I just said something — and the word "egg" spontaneously came out of my mouth. Later I thought: 'That isn't quite right. How can Shih-fu be an egg? But I said it and it's said.'"

When he said "an egg," it was the correct answer. In fact, whatever he said at that moment would have been correct because he did not have any thought in his mind. He was in an absolute state, not making any distinctions. But once he began to entertain doubts, he lost the answer.

Perhaps in this retreat I will also stand in front of you and ask, "Who is standing in front of you?" Then, recalling the story I have just told, you may try to give a similar answer and call Shih-fu a horse. However, this would not be correct if you have the idea of giving a good answer. This is the mind of distinction. It is not the mind that treats everything as equal.

> *Stop activity and return to stillness,*
> *And that stillness will be even more active.*

Originally your mind may be in a relatively stable state. But when you realize that your mind is not completely unmoving, you may try to make it even calmer. However, the effort to still your mind will cause it to become more active. The mind that makes no distinctions is unmoving; there are no ups and downs. If you try to eliminate the ups and downs it would be like observing a pan of water. There are gentle ripples on its surface. But you want the surface to be completely still, so you blow on the water to flatten it out. This creates more ripples. Then you press the water with your hands to stop it from moving. The outcome is even more agitation. If you were to leave the water alone, the ripples would eventually subside and the surface would be still. Common sense tells us that we cannot force the water to become calm. When it comes to practice, however, it is difficult for us to apply the same principle.

When practicing, it is sufficient to just keep your mind on the method. It is unnecessary to reflect upon how well you are doing, or to compare whether you are in a better state now than you were half an hour ago. During the evening talk, I may ask you, "How are you doing today?" At this time you are allowed to express your feelings. But

when you are practicing you should definitely not inves-
tigate your mental state and judge your practice.

Someone said to me, "Shih-fu, I feel very ashamed. I
come to retreat time and again and yet I never make any
progress." I said, "The very fact that you are still coming
to retreat and practicing is proof that you are making
progress."

Practice with an equal mind and don't distinguish
between good and bad. Do not compare your condition
before and after the retreat, or judge whether the method
you are using is right or wrong. If you find you cannot use
the method, you may change it, but first understand why
you cannot use the method. You should not let curiosity
dictate your practice, playing with one method today and
another tomorrow, or switching methods from one sitting
to the next. You should see that there are no real differences between the various methods. Hold on to one
method and go into it as deeply as possible.

This is like your love relationships. When you love
someone, you should persist in that relationship and not
continually change partners. Likewise, keep to one method
and do not keep changing your conception of practice. To
change frequently will give you only trouble.

4
Unifying the Mind

Merely stagnating in duality,
How can you recognize oneness?
If you fail to penetrate oneness,
Both places lose their function.

Whenever you make distinctions, your mind is in opposition. Opposition implies duality. How is this relevant to practice? A practitioner usually wants to attain enlightenment or ultimately, Buddhahood. But this creates a duality of subject and object. The person who is seeking to attain is separate from the attainment, the object of his search. In seeking to become one with the Buddha, he separates himself from it. This is a state of opposition.

Or, perhaps the practitioner knows very well that he has never been separate from the Buddha. But since he has not yet experienced this unity, he seeks the Buddha within himself. Yet even seeking the Buddha within himself creates opposition between his searching mind and the Buddha within. This way, oneness can never be attained.

If that is true, is it correct to practice without seeking anything at all? Every day we chant the Four Great Vows.

The fourth is: I vow to attain Supreme Buddhahood. What is the purpose of chanting this vow if aspiring to attain Buddhahood sets up an opposition? On the other hand, if we do not define our goal, is practice possible?

If you really believe there is no separation, then it is possible to practice without opposition. You must have faith in the fundamental unity to truly begin practicing. However, most people remain in duality. They acknowledge only one God, but they also see themselves as separate from God. There is still a duality. But in Ch'an, at the very beginning of your practice, you must have faith in non-duality. It is the same unity in the *kung-an*[1]: "The myriad dharmas return to one. To what does the One return?" In other words, if all existence comes from one God, where does God come from?

The emphasis of Faith in Mind is on practice. Many of you are practicing counting the breath. The goal of this method is to reach a unified, or single-minded state. After you get to the point where there are no thoughts other than counting, eventually the counting just naturally stops. The numbers disappear, the breath disappears, and the idea of counting the breath is gone. The only thing left is a sense of existence. Using a Ch'an method such as the hua-t'ou may have a similar result in the beginning stages. At a certain point, the hua-t'ou may disappear, or you simply cannot use it anymore. But this does not always mean that you have reached a single-minded state. You may still have the thought of trying to use the hua-t'ou. Only when the thought of practicing is gone will your mind be in a peaceful state of oneness.

A person who has experienced oneness is different from an ordinary person. His faith is stronger than one who can at best intellectually understand what it means to have no distinctions in one's mind. To personally experience it is quite another thing.

In Taoism there is the saying that the one gives rise to the two, and the two give rise to the multiplicity of things. We should not think that the Third Patriarch is confusing Taoism with Buddhism. It is just that he employs Taoist terminology to express the teachings of Buddhism. The highest goal of Taoism is the attainment of the Way, but this is not the same goal as that described in Faith in Mind, for Ch'an transcends oneness. But we must get to the state of oneness before we can go beyond it.

The practice of Ch'an should progress in this sequence: scattered mind, simple mind, one mind, no mind. First we gather our scattered thoughts into a more concentrated, or simple, state of mind. From this concentrated state we can enter the mind of unity. Finally, we leap from the unified mind to the state of no mind. This final process can be accomplished more quickly using the Ch'an methods of hua-t'ou or kung-an.

To go from one mind to no mind does not mean that anything is lost; rather, it means that you are free of the unified state. Someone who dwells in one mind would either be attached to samadhi, or else would feel identified with a certain deity. It is only after you are freed from this unity and enter no mind that you return to your own nature, also called "*wu*," or Ch'an.

Even though this progression in the practice takes

place, while you are actually practicing you should not think to yourself: "I am striving to concentrate my mind. I want to get to the state of one mind, to the state of no mind." If you have such ideas of seeking, you will be in trouble. Just concern yourself with your method; persist with your method to the very end. This in itself is close to a state of unity. If you hold to it, eventually you will reach a point where the method disappears and you will experience one mind.

Once a meditator in his sixties said to me, "Shih-fu, I am very old. I may not have many years left. I really would like to get enlightened as soon as possible. If I don't get enlightened before I die, I will have wasted my life." I said, "Precisely because you are so old you shouldn't have any hopes of getting enlightened. Just practice." The man asked, "How can you tell me to practice and not show me how to get enlightened?" I replied, "If you have the idea of enlightenment, that is already your downfall; you cannot make much progress. If you do nothing but practice, at least you will approach the state of enlightenment. Even if you never get enlightened, the effort is never wasted."

Banish existence and you fall into existence;
Follow emptiness and you turn your back on it.

In the Sung dynasty there was a famous prime minister by the name of Chang Shang-Yin who was opposed to Buddhism. He wrote many essays purporting to refute Buddhism, and he would spend every evening pondering over how he could improve the essay he was then working on.

His wife, observing his obsessive involvement and struggle with his writing, asked him, "What are you doing?" He said, "Buddhism is really hateful. I'm trying to prove there is no Buddha." His wife remarked, "How strange! If you say there is no Buddha, why bother to refute the Buddha? It is as if you are throwing punches into empty space."

This comment turned his mind around. He reflected: There may be something to Buddhism after all. So he started studying Buddhism and became a well-known, accomplished lay practitioner of Ch'an. In fact, Chang Shang-Yin and Ch'an master Ta-Hui Tsung-Kao[2] had the same master, Yuan-Wu K'o-Ch'in.

Thus if you try to destroy something, you are still bound up by it. For instance, suppose you try to clear a blocked pipe by pushing another object into it. Whatever was originally in the pipe is pushed out, but the new object is now blocking the pipe. When you try to use existence to get rid of existence, you will always end up with existence.

When you throw something away, it is gone. But does it cease to exist? In local terms, yes. In the broader picture, however, that is not the case. On this earth, no matter how hard you try to throw anything away, it will still stay somewhere on the earth.

There is a Chinese novel called *Monkey*. The hero is a "supermonkey" who is so powerful that he can travel a distance of 180,000 miles in one somersault. In the story, he was journeying to the Western Paradise of Amitabha Buddha. On the way, he came upon five tall mountain peaks. He figured that it would take one leap to get to the other side. First he took a rest, urinating at that spot. Then he somersaulted over the mountains. After he landed, he noticed a funny smell. He thought, "Some shameless monkey must have taken a leak here." Actually, he had never gotten to the other side of the mountains. He had just somersaulted back to the original spot.

The five mountains in the story symbolize the five *skandhas*[3] within which sentient beings are trapped. All of your actions will boomerang back to you and you will have to take the consequences. If you throw anything away, it will be you who has to clean it up. You may think that you can avoid responsibility by passing it on to another person. In the short term, it may work. But ultimately, you have to deal with it yourself, and in addition, you have caused trouble to others.

Therefore you should not try to get rid of your vexations. Rather, you should be willing to accept them. Once someone said, "Shih-fu, my karmic obstructions are too great. Please recite mantras to remove them from me." I replied, "And what will happen to these karmic obstructions when I remove them from you? Should they become Shih-fu's?" If you have difficulties you should not consider them problems. If you are obsessed with these difficulties and try to eliminate them, you are only getting yourself into greater trouble.

Those who have just begun to practice experience many problems with their bodies and minds. They are constantly saying, "I have to overcome all these problems." But in trying to eliminate their problems, they struggle. This is what is meant by "Banish existence and you fall into existence."

The second line, "Follow emptiness and you turn your back on it," refers to practitioners who have experienced certain breakthroughs, and are approaching the state of emptiness. They may think, "I have eliminated all vexations. I no longer have any ignorance or attachment." But staying at this level would be considered "outer path" practice. The best these practitioners can do is reach the emptiness samadhi, the highest level of the formless realm.

I have known many people who were extremely diligent and took their practice very seriously in the beginning, but gave up too soon. It is just as if when one side senses it is losing the battle, suddenly all resistance is gone and they are defeated very quickly. As long as everything is going well, they continue normally; but as soon as something goes wrong, everything simply collapses. So it is with certain practitioners who have been working hard and then suddenly stop completely. They feel that practice is basically useless. They think it is a great deception, because they have put a lot of energy into overcoming their problems, and have not eliminated them at all. In fact, their efforts have only increased their mental vexations, and have created physical ones as well.

Because of this, many people consider serious or energetic practice demonic. They think it is not normal to devote oneself so completely to practice. Such criticism is usually unjustified. However, it is true that a practitioner who does not know what he is doing may get into deep trouble, especially without proper guidance. He may not be in a demonic state, but very likely his practice cannot last long.

It is good to have a diligent and objective attitude towards practice. But to be attached to the idea of overcoming your problems will only lead to further trouble.

(1) *kung-an:* (Japanese: *koan*). Literally, a "public case," a Ch'an method of meditation in which the practitioner energetically and single-mindedly pursues the answer to an enigmatic question posed by the master, or ponders the meaning of a famous recorded encounter between a master and disciple of the past.

(2) Ta-Hui Tsung-Kao (1089-1163), known as the greatest advocate of *kung-an* practice, is often contrasted with his contemporary, Hung-Chih Cheng-Chueh, the greatest teacher of the silent illumination method. More disciples were enlightened under Ta-Hui than any other Ch'an master, and he is also noted for spreading the teachings of Ch'an among the laity. A compilation of his writings and talks is available in English under the title *Swampland Flowers.*

(3) the five *skandhas:* the five categories, or "heaps," of existence — form, sensation, perception, volition, and consciousness.

5
Stilling Words and Thoughts

Excessive talking and thinking
Turn you from harmony with the Way.
Cut off talking and thinking,
And there is nowhere you cannot penetrate.

People like to talk, especially if they feel lonely. Those who tend to talk non-stop generally have difficulty with practice, and also make it difficult for others to practice. In our Ch'an retreat, talking is forbidden, but there are still some people who cannot resist covertly saying a few words. Others honor the rule and refrain from speaking, but that does not mean that they are not talking to themselves. All day long, while they are sitting, they come up with a theme, and then carry on a conversation with themselves. They ponder over all sorts of issues.

Once a certain writer attended a retreat. During the first day, he came up with the idea for a novel. While sitting, he sketched out the plot and the various characters. In the private interview the next day I asked him how he had been doing, and he said, "I've been making plans for my new novel." I said to him, "Perhaps you should go home and start writing your novel now. Otherwise, by the end of the retreat you will have forgotten all the great ideas you have come up with."

If you talk too much, either with your mouth or in your head, it will be difficult to make progress. When you find it hard to concentrate, it is very easy to start talking to yourself. You may not even be able to control it.

There is a deeper interpretation of these four lines. You should not try to use logic or theory to answer certain questions in your practice. Some examples are: "Why have I come here for a retreat?" "What is the purpose of practice?" "What is enlightenment?" If you get involved in this kind of questioning to justify your practice, then you simply cannot practice.

After a few days of practice, many people completely stop thinking about themselves and their outside affairs. However, they keep dwelling on my words. Whatever I say is meant to guide your practice, but when you are actually practicing, you should just use the method and not think about what I may have said. The less you talk to yourself, the closer you will be to the highest Way.

I once told a student, "You really have to practice very hard to overcome ignorance." For two sitting periods she was constantly thinking, "How am I ignorant?" Unable to contain it any longer, she got up and said to me, "I can eat. I can sleep. So I am really not ignorant." I said, "Look at a dog, a cat, a mosquito. They can eat and rest. Are you saying that they don't have any ignorance?" Then she said, "Tell me what to do so that I won't be ignorant." I said, "Try to meditate and recite the Buddha's name." She went back to her cushion and meditated on the Buddha's name. But again, she thought to herself: "Since I am here meditating and reciting the Buddha's name, I am not ignorant." After another two periods, she came to me again and said, "In fact, I don't have any problems. I have been sitting here feeling very comfortable. It is you who have vexations." Her problem was that although she took my words seriously, she would turn them over and over in her mind instead of actually applying the method during practice.

It is only when you no longer have any words or thoughts that the perfect Way will manifest before you, and "there is nowhere you cannot penetrate." The meaning is not that you can go anywhere, but that there is no need to go anywhere, because in the state of no words and no thoughts you are in the midst of anywhere and every place. How do you get to the state of no words and no thoughts? By picking up the method and putting down your attachment to other things.

> *Return to the root and attain the principle;*
> *Pursue illumination and you lose it.*
> *One moment of reversing the light*
> *Is greater than the previous emptiness.*

In practice, you may try to penetrate to the emptiness of phenomena. But as long as illumination is directed towards outward appearances, you miss the primal source. It is only by turning the illumination inward that you return to the source, and get to the meaning of all things. If you can do this even for a split second, you will transcend the state of emptiness.

The source, or root, is Buddha nature. How do you return to the root? By letting go of all words and thoughts and eliminating all grasping and rejection. You must begin with a method, but at some point you must let it go. Likewise, you should not hold on to any experiences that may come up. When the method and experiences are no longer necessary to you, you will have returned to the source. This source, or Buddha nature, is the lively manifestation of great liberation and great wisdom. In great liberation, there is nothing left. But this is not the same as "stubborn emptiness." Liberation goes beyond both emptiness and form.

The previous emptiness is transformed;
It was all a product of deluded views.

Practitioners often go from attachment to existence, to attachment to emptiness. If one thinks that emptiness is true wisdom or liberation, under this delusion, one cannot attain the ultimate. It is natural for people to become attached to their experiences. One student who sat very well last night tried to repeat the experience today by recalling exactly what he did that resulted in that great sitting. But today the sitting went very poorly. This was due to his greed for the experience.

No need to seek the real;
Just extinguish your views.

We should not seek Buddha nature or enlightenment; rather, we should let it come about naturally. Such questions as "When will I get enlightened?" or "Is there a Buddha nature?" will take you even farther away from Buddha nature, which is a totality and not something you can grasp. Buddha nature is in the totality of your own self. Why should it be necessary to try to attain it? And how can you get hold of it? Don't practice with the thought of reaching Buddhahood, just put forth your best efforts.

Retreat Two

December 25, 1984 – January 1, 1985

6
Giving Up Expectations

Do not abide in dualistic views;
Take care not to seek after them.
As soon as there is right and wrong
The mind is scattered and lost.

Dualistic views refer to the discriminating mind. They include any doubts about the correctness of your method, or whether your decision to attend this retreat was a right or a wrong one. If you lack faith, you will doubt the method you are using. On the other hand, if your confidence is too strong, then you will be expecting something out of the practice. Neither extreme is beneficial.

To come to a retreat merely out of curiosity shows a lack of faith in yourself and in the practice; it would be impossible for you to get good results. From the very beginning you are denying yourself the possibility of doing well on retreat. At the same time, you may harbor certain resentments: you may get annoyed at the people around you, or even at your own body when your legs cause you pain. You may be critical of the food, or the style of the retreat.

Having too much faith in yourself is likewise a problem. Someone who was extremely confident came to one retreat. He was highly intelligent, and a top student. He thought: "If a person like me cannot get enlightened, then who can?" After one day of practice, his back ached, his legs hurt, and he began to question if this was the way to get enlightened. One evening in the Ch'an hall, he heard me say, "If you can do it, sit through the night." He concluded that in order to get enlightened, he should forgo sleep. By midnight his eyes were heavy, but he forced himself to continue sitting. After three days of this, he was totally exhausted and he said to me, "Now I have some idea of this enlightenment you are talking about. Basically you just have to go without sleep."

Practice is like cooking rice. If you use a gentle flame the rice will be perfect and easy to digest, whereas with a high flame, it will burn before it is done. One should practice with a very relaxed attitude.

If you do not abide in duality, neither having too much nor too little confidence, then what should you do? You have not come here to get enlightened, but to practice. It is not important whether you have a good grasp of the matter and can enter the practice deeply or not. Just do not have any doubts about the method or whether you have the "right stuff" to practice. Do not underestimate yourself. If others can practice, then at least you can try.

Once a student who did well on her first retreat came a second time. At first everything went fine, but then a problem arose. While sitting it occurred to her that counting the breath was really boring. If she spent her time reciting the name of the Buddha, she thought, then at least she would be accumulating merit. But what was the use of counting from one to ten? Towards evening she said to me, "Shih-fu, I don't want to stay on this retreat. One-two-three-four-five-six-seven-eight-nine-ten. Even a kid in kindergarten can do that. Why should I waste my time here?"

When your mind strays from the method, problems will appear. In fact, the method is inherently meaningless. It is irrelevant to discuss whether it brings merit or not. The purpose of a method is to train your mind. You can raise the same objection about prostrating to the Buddha, or morning and evening chanting. Why should practice take these forms?

People often wonder: If Ch'an is a method of sudden enlightenment which does not depend on meditation, then why do we practice meditation and go on seven-day retreats? If someone objects that these things are unrelated to Ch'an, I say that if you want to study Ch'an I will instruct you in exactly these methods. In order to practice, you must believe in your teacher and in his methods. If you search for methods on your own, you may not find anything and eventually give up practicing. Or you may find something weird and end up in a demonic state, with mental and physical problems.

Someone once said to me, "I only believe in ancient Ch'an." I asked, "What do you mean by 'ancient Ch'an'?" He replied, "Whereas the so-called Ch'an masters of today teach people to meditate, ancient Ch'an does not require any practice. My enlightenment experience came from the ancient, direct method, without any practice. I have been to many masters looking for one who would confirm my experience. Unfortunately, I have been unsuccessful so far." He was not actually interested in studying with a master, but in obtaining the credentials to spread the Dharma on his own. After a brief conversation, I realized that this person was not quite straight in his mind, and said to him, "I am not enlightened myself, so how can I tell whether you are enlightened or not?" He said, "Strange. If you say you are not enlightened, then how can you teach Ch'an?" I said, "I may not be enlightened myself, but I can teach others to get enlightened. For example, it is not necessary for a cardiologist to have heart problems to treat others successfully." He said, "In that case, am I capable of teaching Ch'an to others?" I replied, "Since I don't know anything about you I can't answer that question."

Meditation should just be a part of life. If you have other motivations, it will lead to problems. When you approach the practice with any expectations, you will not be able to sit well. Not only should you not have any expectations of getting enlightened or becoming a Ch'an master, but you should not even expect to be free from your pain. Do not hope that your legs or back will stop hurting. Do not try to overcome the pain as if you had to burst through a barrier. Simply accept the pain. You may not feel very happy about it, but at least do not resent it. If you cannot accept it, then ignore it and turn your mind to the method. When the pain becomes too great to ignore, place your attention on the pain itself. Disassociate yourself from the part of your body that is painful. Let it ache away. If you can take this attitude, eventually it will go away. When you really get into the practice, all bodily sensation will disappear.

The important thing is not to have any resentment against your suffering, or any expectations of happiness. As soon as ideas such as suffering versus happiness arise, your mind will already be straying from the method, caught up in duality.

You are all aware that this Center is not an ideal environment for practice. The neighbors hammer against the walls. Outside there is a continual stream of traffic and airplanes passing overhead. Yet even in the midst of this noisy and crowded world we are given a small area to practice. So we should not let our minds be distracted by what is going on outside or by what comes in contact with our senses.

On retreat you are living with many people which may create an uncomfortable environment. You don't feel free or find it as convenient as at home. On the other hand, the presence of others will encourage, almost force you to practice. Even if you are not practicing energetically, at least you will make an effort to appear to be practicing.

When people sit together, they can be of great benefit to each other. Whether you practice well or not, treasure this rare opportunity and do your best.

7
Beyond One Mind

Two comes from one,
Yet do not even keep the one.
When one mind does not arise,
Myriad dharmas are without defect.

In yesterday's talk I cautioned against abiding in duality. Although we should not abide in duality, we still must hold on to the method. Method is that which helps us to unify our minds, to replace the constant stream of scattered thoughts. After the mind is concentrated by the method, we eventually reach a point where the method itself disappears and the mind is one. Today someone said during the interview, "I have been practicing for quite a few years but I have never had the experience of forgetting my body, or my method disappearing." I said, "You should not be too anxious about it. Just proceed naturally." The state of one mind has to come about naturally. Naturally, the method will leave you behind; it is not for you to think of leaving the method behind. The state of one mind is not easy to attain. But today I will go one step further and say that even the one mind has to be transcended and left behind.

In the *Avatamsaka Sutra* there are the following two lines: "With no exception everything comes from the Dharma Realm. With no exception everything will return to the Dharma Realm." Everything is generated by the one and will eventually return to the one. This concept can be found in both oriental and western philosophy. But in Buddha Dharma even that state is not good enough.

A disciple of Chao-Chou once asked his master, "If the myriad dharmas[1] return to one, to what does the one return?" Chao-Chou answered, "In Ch'ing-chou I had a robe made, weighing seven pounds."

To be attached to the one can either take the form of pure materialism or monotheism. But in the course of practice it is necessary to first get to the one. It is only then that you realize that even this one is not ultimate. It is still on a worldly level. Only when you can transcend this unified state will you reach genuine Buddha Dharma.

You begin by concentrating the scattered mind. To say that the mind is concentrated does not mean that it is in a unified state, because there is still a distinction between subject and object, between you and the method. But when the method drops away, your mind will be very clear, without any thoughts, and you are left only with a sense of your own existence. This is the state of one mind, also called samadhi. However, this is only an elementary level of samadhi, and if you continue on the same course you can get into ever-deepening samadhi states. However, Ch'an practitioners do not dwell in samadhi, but attempt to drop even that state of one mind.

Today a student mentioned that when he sits he very often enters a very comfortable, enjoyable state. This type of sensation is really an expression of desire. As long as a person is attached to a desire for bodily or mental pleasure of any kind, there is no hope of entering into one mind. This is because your mind is divided into two, or even three: a sense of your self, of your body, and of the pleasure. If a pleasurable sensation arises while sitting, you should remain aloof from it. Yet this experience is not completely useless, because it at least motivates you to continue practicing and to attend retreats. Indeed, an enjoyable meditation experience can exceed the pleasure that derives from food or sex. But as soon as you reach this stage, leave it behind.

Another term for one mind is "great self," because although the mind is enormously expanded, there is still a sense of self-centeredness, or "I." So long as you are attached to "I," there can be no liberation. If you feel that you are abiding in a state of "perfection," or think of yourself as a perfect master, this is at best the great self.

Thus there are two meanings of "one" referred to in this line: "Yet do not even keep the one." The first is samadhi and the second is the great self. These are the highest states that can be attained from the practice of worldly dharma. From the point of view of Ch'an, even though a person may reach samadhi or the great self, he will still be in samsara, the cycle of birth and death. The liberation that he feels is only transitory; it is not ultimate liberation. But "When one mind does not arise, myriad dharmas are without defect." That is to say, a person in the state of one mind is still subject to problems, but when he loses even that one mind nothing can cause him any trouble.

One thing should be clarified here. In the state of one mind, there are no vexations. Trouble can only develop in a state of discrimination. As long as you stay in a state of one mind, nothing can bother, tempt, or excite you. The problem with one mind is that it cannot last forever; inevitably, a thought will arise, and it will evolve into two, three, and many. The state of one can only be considered in relation to two. A true totality would not even be considered "one"; it can only be called "nothing." It is only when a distinction is made that the one can exist at all, and in that case it will lead to two. You can only feel lonely when you are aware of the possible existence of another person. In complete totality, there is no sense of loneliness.

> *Without defect, without dharmas,*
> *No arising, no mind.*

No mind, or Ch'an, is a state of non-arising and non-perishing. Not a single thought will arise, and even that unmoving mind fundamentally does not exist. There is nothing that can give you trouble, and nothing that you can give trouble to.

Both our body and mind need food to survive. There are two types of food for the body: nutrition and contact. "Contact food" includes the sensation of touching another person, and the feeling of changing into clean clothes after a shower. There is another kind of food for the mind, called "consciousness food," which satisfies the ordinary minds' hunger for experience and phenomena. If you can leave the first two kinds of food, you will be outside of the desire realm. But beyond the desire realm, there are the form realm and the formless realm. To go beyond them, you have to free yourself from the food of consciousness. In the state of one mind, where only consciousness exists, you may have transcended the desire realm but are still in samsara. Only when you are free from all three types of food will you enter no mind, and be outside samsaric realms.

(1) dharma: a "thing" or "object," a physical or mental phenomenon. Capitalized, Dharma refers to the Buddhist "Law" or "teaching."

8
Illusions

The subject is extinguished with the object.
The object sinks away with the subject.

The mind dharma cannot arise by itself or function alone. It always co-exists with the form dharma. The Zen expression "one hand clapping" illustrates the impossibility of such a thing. The mind can only be found in the realm of mental objects.

Once Master Nan-Ch'uan went to the farm of the monastery where he was abbot. The previous night, a local earth deity informed the farmers of Nan-Ch'uan's impending visit, so they had prepared a welcome feast. He asked them, "How did you know I was coming?" They answered, "Last night the earth deity told us you were coming today." Upon hearing this, the master said, "I am really very ashamed. My practice must be quite poor that even deities manage to peep into my mind." He meant that when he thought of going to the farm, the mind dharma had arisen in conjunction with the form dharma, or the concrete idea of the farm. When his mind moved, the deity was able to see it.

The same master was meditating in a hut next to a river. One night he heard two ghosts conversing. One of them was rejoicing that his term was coming to an end because the next day someone would be replacing him. The second ghost asked, "Who will be replacing you?" He replied, "A man wearing an iron hat." The master wondered to himself who this person could be. The next day there was heavy rain and the river rose to a higher level. The master looked out of his hut and saw a man about to cross the river. He had covered his head with a wok for protection against the rain. Immediately, the master knew that this was the man of the iron hat, so he cautioned him saying, "Don't cross the river today. It's too dangerous." The man asked, "Why?" "Because the water is very deep and running rapidly." The man listened to the old monk's advice and returned home.

You must understand that in Chinese lore, water ghosts are prisoners until another person drowns and takes their place. That night as he was meditating, the master heard the two ghosts again. This time the first ghost was complaining, "I have been stuck here for so many years, and I thought my chance for freedom had finally come. But now the old monk interfered and messed everything up. I'll show him what I can do." With that, the ghost broke a hole in the bank of the river, so that the water would run down and cover the hut. The master realized that the ghost was trying to drown him. Suddenly he disappeared from sight. The ghost looked around, but the hut was empty.

Actually, the master was still there and heard the ghost very clearly. He was invisible for the simple reason that his mind was not moving. It was not influenced by the environment, no longer tied to mental objects, which are shadows of the mind.

All of our thoughts are illusory; they depend on certain objects or symbols. If there are no objects, forms or symbols in your mind, there would be no illusory thoughts. It is possible, however, to have an illusory thought that is considered "right thought" if you maintain this one thought continually without interference. For instance, counting the breath is in itself an illusory thought, but if you maintain it without a break it would be the right thought, the method of your practice.

On the other hand, if your thoughts are constantly changing, they would be considered "wandering thoughts" rather than "right thought." But both of these situations are not the pure mind because your mind is still attached to mental realms. It is not the state of no mind; it is not even the state of one mind. With these mental objects in your mind it would be difficult to control your next birth at the time of death. Instead, where you go will be directed by the thrust of your karma. Karma leads you in the direction of your strongest desire or attachment. Thus your mind follows the mental realm that you are most attracted to. If your mind is free from the environment, not bounded by mental realms, then your next birth will not be dictated by karma but rather by your own decision. Being free to go wherever you wish, you are outside of the cycle of birth and death.

So long as your mind is filled with greed, hatred, or ignorance, you will be immersed in vexation and suffering. You will not even be reborn in the heavens, not to mention be liberated from birth and death. Heavenly states can only be attained by performing meritorious deeds with a minimum of desire. And you could not reach one mind, or samadhi, because of your strong attachment to certain objects.

Thus when you are practicing, all thoughts other than the method should be considered as demons, even if it feels like you have entered a "heavenly" state. Some people, as they are sitting, may suddenly enter a completely new world which is very beautiful and comfortable. Afterwards, they want to return to it in each meditation. They may be able to get into that state again, but nonetheless it is an attachment. There are also other states that are terrifying. Such visions, good and bad, are generally manifestations of our own mental realms.

Now we can understand why the methods of kung-an and hua-t'ou are different than counting the breath, reciting the Buddha's name, or repeating a mantra. Though the latter are necessary in the beginning, they include relative objects (i.e. the breath, the Buddha's name, or the mantra). In these cases, the objects make up your mental realm. And where there is an object there must be a subject, namely, the self. But kung-an and hua-t'ou are objectless methods of practice. Other than the method, there is nothing in front of you. For example, the question "What is *wu*?"[1] does not have an answer you can grasp. There is nothing behind the question. You are just using it as a method to practice. If there is no object, then what about a subject? When you enter deeply into this method, even though you may not be enlightened, you will not have any sense of self. Your entire self will be enclosed in a great mass of doubt. No ghosts or deities would be able to find you.

(1) "What is *wu*?": (*wu*=Chinese, "nothing" or "there is not"; in Japanese, *mu*). Hua-t'ou based on the kung-an in which Master Chao-Chou was asked by a monk, "Does a dog have Buddha nature?", to which Chao-Chou replied, "*Wu.*" Alteratively practiced by just looking into the word *wu/mu*.

9
Awareness of Vexations

Object is object because of the subject;
Subject is subject because of the object.
Know that the two
Are originally one emptiness.
In one emptiness the two are the same,
Containing all phenomena.

These lines describe a non-discriminating mind in which, nevertheless, there is perfectly clear discrimination.

In the course of practice, the more negative things you discover about yourself, the clearer you will be as to the road you should walk.

After leaving mainland China, I was conscripted into the Nationalist army in Taiwan. At that time, everything was in a state of confusion and the troops were crowded together in a warehouse. In this warehouse there were no windows or lights, and at night people couldn't see their way to the toilet so many just relieved themselves where they were. Others who decided to feel their way outside ended up stepping on the mess in the dark. However, at daybreak one could see the shit very clearly and avoid it.

It was a mistake to imagine that just because you couldn't see it, there was no shit on the floor.

Those who have never taken up the practice are like the people in that dark room. No matter where they walk, they step into shit. Coming to retreat is like putting a light into the room. Maybe the light will only stay on for a minute, but at least you can see some of the problem areas. Gradually, you will be able to tell exactly where the shit is and where it isn't. The more you know, the less likely you will step in it. But to get angry when you discover problems would just be adding trouble to trouble. It would be as if, after realizing you stepped on some shit, you did it again just to punish yourself.

Retreats are like road repair. When there is a problem underneath the road, the workers break up the pavement in order to fix the cables, pipes, or whatever is faulty. After they finish the work, they pave over it again and everything is just as it was before. Likewise, in order to make our own repairs, we have to break up the road and mess things up temporarily. Thus discovering one's problems in the course of practice is very useful, but do these problems actually exist?

Yes, the miseries of the retreat are quite real. You are truly tired and uncomfortable. You are definitely in this place and not some other. Yet you must look at non-existence from the point of view of existence. When you can't concentrate on the method, when you haven't gotten enough sleep, and when your legs are painful, it is all really happening. But originally your legs were not painful. It was only after you started sitting that they became painful. If you stretch out your legs they will no longer be painful. Thus when you experience pain you should keep in mind that it doesn't have a true existence. If it did, it would be there even when you were not meditating.

Though some of you have trouble concentrating, it cannot be that during the entire retreat there has not been at least once when you could concentrate to some extent. If you can use your method even for a very short time, that already lets you know that your scattered mind does not have true existence. Do not be fearful when your mind is scattered; just recognize that it is temporary.

But when you succeed in concentrating, is that mind real? Of course not. If the mind were truly concentrated, it could not become scattered again. Now if both the scattered mind and the concentrated mind are unreal, that means there is originally no mind. If this is so, it should be very easy to progress in the practice. To be aware that mind does not exist will strengthen your faith, even though you have not experienced no mind. So long as you have faith in the non-existence of mind you can keep on practicing without any anxiety or disappointment.

A small setback does not mean that you have failed; it is just that the time has not yet arrived. If you climb half-way up a mountain, you cannot say that you have failed. You just need to continue climbing until you reach the summit. One time I was in a car with a few people, driving up a mountain. After two hours, I asked the driver, "What's going on? We don't seem to be getting anywhere on this mountain." He said, "Actually, we have reached the top. It was a very flat, gradual rise."

Now let us look at existence from the point of view of emptiness. For example, a monk cannot say that women do not exist just because he does not have relationships with them. There is a story I often tell from the kung-ans. A monk who was practicing Ch'an was being supported by an old woman, who provided him with a hut and daily offerings of food. One day she decided to test his practice. She told her beautiful daughter to bring the monk his food, and then embrace him. The next day, the old woman asked the monk, "How did you find my daughter?" He replied, "Like dry wood leaning against a cold rock." With that, she grabbed a broom and shooed him away, saying, "All this time I thought you were a man of Ch'an!"

Although this monk had reached a deep level of practice, he had not yet realized Ch'an. Being attached to emptiness, he denied existence. During a retreat, you can enter a state where you do not taste your food or know where you are walking. You do not recognize the person you are looking at. In this condition, your body follows the normal routine, but your mind is totally absorbed in the method. You have entered the great doubt sensation.

Prior to this, when your mind is still scattered, I tell you to concentrate carefully on whatever you are doing, and to maintain a total awareness of every action. When you are completely focused, you may slip into the next stage, where you lose awareness of your body, even as it continues to function smoothly and automatically.

The third level is a return to total awareness. However, unlike the first level, there are no scattered thoughts whatsoever. When you are eating, you are just eating. When you are sleeping, you are just sleeping. No more, no less.

Originally you had to work very hard on your method, but when you get to the second level, everything flows naturally. The practice just keeps moving like a ball rolling down a hill. At that time, even though you are practicing very well, you would not think of yourself as practicing. This is called the true existence of emptiness. That is to say, you feel that nothing exists, but your mind is really there, working on the method. The experience of one's method and body disappearing can be due to two factors. On the one hand, one can slip into a kind of nebulous state out of pure laziness. On the other hand, a person using the method very well is just like someone so accustomed to riding a horse that they forget the horse beneath them. This is a good phenomenon.

A person who has arrived at enlightened mind is looking at existence from the standpoint of emptiness. Once a Ch'an master was asked by his disciple, "If many calamities were to appear before you at once, what would you do?" The master answered, "Red is not white and green is not yellow. Whatever it is, that's what it is." But isn't seeing whatever a thing is the way everybody sees things?

During the Sung Dynasty, China was invaded by the Mongols. When a band of warriors descended on a certain town, everyone fled, including the soldiers and the monks in the temples. When the Mongols entered the gates, they found that one Ch'an master had remained. Thinking that he stayed behind as part of a plot, they brought him before their general. When asked why he did not flee, he said,

"Everybody has to die sometime. I could die here. I could die there. Why should I flee?" The general asked, "You are not afraid of death?" The monk replied, "I would not say that I am hoping to die. But if my time has come, then that's that." The general said, "I'm going to kill you." The monk replied, "All right. But I want to tell you something first. Don't think that you are killing me. Is your sword capable of killing wind or water? If you slice into water, you just separate it for an instant and then it comes together again. If you cut off my head, you just separate it from my body, but your killing me is your own business. It has nothing to do with me, because I neither desire nor fear death." That is to say, after enlightenment everything exists, but not the self.

We have talked of emptiness from the point of view of existence and existence from the point of view of emptiness. Both existence and emptiness are existing and non-existing. Do you understand? Don't worry if you don't. If you truly grasp the meaning, you are already enlightened.

10
Making Comparisons

Not seeing fine or coarse,
How can there be any bias?

"Fine or coarse" refers to the deepness or shallowness of practice. I have often cautioned you against comparing your practice with that of others or your own self at different times. Such comparisons are only subjective. Today someone burst out crying in the meditation hall. One person may have thought, "Oh, she's not doing so well." Another, "I think she's becoming enlightened!" Or else, "Maybe she's going crazy." None of these thoughts may represent the true situation. Whether she felt pain or sorrow, became enlightened, or went crazy, it's her business. It has nothing to do with anyone else. Making comparisons inevitably means judging others.

When you are sitting, refrain from looking around and sizing people up. A common type of comparison people make on retreat is to see someone sitting through three periods and think, "How can he do that? Don't his legs hurt? Boy! My legs hurt all the time. I can barely get through one period." Sometime later, the person does move a little and they say to themselves, "Ha! Probably his legs are hurting now. So he's not so special after all."

These are examples of comparing yourself to others, but you can also compare yourself to yourself. Perhaps you are having a miserable time from day one. Your legs hurt, you are generally uncomfortable and cannot get into the spirit of practice. You feel plagued with problems, but there comes a day when suddenly you feel great. Your body is comfortable and your mind is calm. You are pleased by this change of affairs and say to yourself, "I finally got it." You have become so excited, you can no longer meditate. Later when your meditation is not as pleasurable, you may try to analyze how you sat so well that one time and why you are so uncomfortable now.

Comparing good and bad is just deluded thinking. As long as you are immersed in these wandering thoughts, you will not enter the proper conditions for practice. Do not concern yourself with anything going on around you. Nor should you be concerned with anything going on inside yourself. Focus fully on the method and do not make external or internal comparisons. If you can do that, your practice will be effective.

On the first night, I said that you must begin by isolating yourself. There are four stages of progressive isolation. First, isolate yourself from your affairs outside the retreat. Next, ignore the environment within the retreat itself. As far as you are concerned, you are the only person here. Take another step further and put aside all thoughts of the past and future. Finally, forget the thought that has just passed or the thought to come. Narrow yourself down to the thought of the present moment. You are reduced to a tiny, tiny point, which is concentrated on the method. Even so, a demon can come and grab you, because you still have that miniscule point left. But if you can continue to focus on the method single-mindedly, it will be easy for you to depart from even that one thought.

No matter how disturbing your surroundings or your inner mind, you should take clear note of it and avoid feeling any aversion. Any feelings of good or bad regarding the environment or ourselves are actually projections of our own deep-seated emotional attachments. Events and things have no intrinsic good or evil qualities.

For instance, this incense board is just a piece of wood. There is nothing good or bad about it, but when an inexperienced monitor hits someone in the wrong place — say, the neck or shoulder blade — the person may react to the board in a negative way. The monitor may also blame the incense board for being awkward to use. But someone who is hit by an adept monitor will feel very good and consider the board a great help. Likewise, the monitor may think that this is a particularly good incense board since it is easy to wield.

Today I cut my finger trying to open a stuck window. I may have thought that something was wrong with the window, but the window is an inert object. It is not its fault that I hurt my finger. Perhaps I should blame my hand instead, but a hand is only flesh and bone. When flesh and bone are applied to a window, there is nothing in that event itself that can be called good or bad.

The enlightened individual does not see things as bad, good, coarse or fine. There are no good or bad people in the world. Someone may think, "If a good person is the same as a bad person, wouldn't this create a lot of confusion?" This problem does not arise for one who is deeply enlightened. In the past, those who attained great enlightenment had strong hearts of compassion. They dedicated the remainder of their lives to saving other living beings. Sakyamuni Buddha himself devoted forty-odd years to teaching and saving sentient beings. It is not that the Buddha wants to save sentient beings. It is just that sentient beings need to be saved. Whether or not he saves particular beings is not up to him, but up to the beings themselves. If there are beings that are capable of being saved, then the Buddha saves them. If there are those who are too difficult to save, then he does not save them. He does not blame them for being too difficult to save, nor does he condemn them to hell. This is not the attitude of the Buddha or the patriarchs.

The Buddha's response to sentient beings can be likened to a mirror. In itself, a mirror contains no image or particular characteristic. It merely reflects whatever you put in front of it, as it is, without hindrance. Likewise, the Buddha teaches people according to their differing requirements. If someone needs a demon, a demon will appear; if they need the Buddha, then the Buddha will appear; if someone needs Ch'an practice, then Ch'an methods appear. The Buddha does not conceive these things and try to push them on others. Rather, his compassionate response is just an automatic reflection of a person's own mind.

This is why there are various levels in Buddhism. It is a recognition of the many different capacities of sentient beings. Whatever an individual's tendency, they can find a level of the teachings that is right for them.

One who is really involved in the practice becomes like a mirror, without discrimination or biases. When you reach the point where the method disappears and even you disappear, your mind will be a mirror — containing nothing, reflecting perfectly.

> *The Great Way is broad,*
> *Neither easy nor difficult.*

The purpose of using Ch'an methods in training students is to sweep away any attachments that remain in their minds. If they desire to attain Buddhahood, the master may say, "There is no Buddha." No doubt, it is necessary to have a certain attachment to the method, to gain some result, such as samadhi or enlightenment. But when your mind is a steady stream, uninterrupted by extraneous thoughts, the Ch'an master will push you to let go of the idea of practice, to break your attachment to striving for an end.

There are a few stories of Ch'an patriarchs and their students which illustrate this. One student went up to his teacher and said, "I want to practice to attain the Way." The teacher said, "There is no Way to be attained by practice." Another student declared, "I want to attain liberation." His teacher replied, "Who is holding you back?" There was a student who said, "I have heard it said that Sakyamuni Buddha left home, practiced for many years, and attained enlightenment." His teacher commented, "Hah. What a pity. If I had seen him, I would have given him a good beating and thrown him to the dogs."

You may think that these teachers are destroying Buddhism by making such statements. But actually they are working to remove even the slightest attachment in the student's mind. When a person really understands what it is to have a mind free of discrimination, he can be considered capable of practice. To reach this point, faith is of the utmost importance. Some may think, "Sakyamuni Buddha and the patriarchs left the home life and cultivated for many years before they attained enlightenment. As for me, I don't think I'm up to becoming a monk (or a nun.) So what's the use of practicing?" If you consider practice to be difficult and painful, then practice is difficult and painful. But if you consider it easy, then it's very easy. Practice itself is neither difficult nor easy. As I said before, there is nothing inherently good or bad in events themselves. Discriminations of good and bad, difficult and easy, are in our own minds and have nothing to do with the phenomenon itself.

Someone asked me how you can be concerned about alleviating suffering if you hold the concept that there is nothing really good or bad. An illustration I gave previously may explain it. While you are sitting, your leg becomes painful. But as soon as you stretch it out, the pain goes away. There is no question that it hurts, but the pain is not real because it does not endure. It is capable of changing and disappearing. It is the same with good and bad. They are subject to change. Bad can become good.

That bad exists is only a particular way of seeing and dealing with things. Pain is still pain, but what is important is your understanding of its nature. From that perspective, you can learn to alleviate your own suffering. When it comes to seeing the suffering of others, you can reflect on your own experience. Even though you tell yourself that suffering is empty, you still feel pain. Likewise, in teaching others, even though you may say that suffering is non-existent, you cannot deny their experience of suffering. As far as they are concerned, pain is direct and real. Thus, from the perspective that suffering is unreal, you still respond to that unreal experience. You strive out of compassion to alleviate the suffering of others.

There are two ways of understanding that practice is neither difficult nor easy. A beginning practitioner can only understand it intellectually. He may believe that practice is neither difficult nor easy, but this is quite different from knowing directly through experience that difficulties are just fabricated by the mind. There is nothing difficult about practice itself. The individuals themselves bring difficulty to the practice. During retreat, one person may find practice extremely difficult, and another may find it easy. It can even be different for the same person at different times. It has to do with our mental attitude, or the way we approach it.

People respond to difficulty in different ways. Some people become so overwhelmed by troubles in their practice, they end up without any discrimination, letting go of their hopes as well as their despair. As a result, the instant they turn their minds towards practice, they get a good result. Although this may happen, it is not the case that everybody needs to go through the same kind of process. In fact, when some people encounter trouble, it does not reinforce their practice at all. On the contrary, they are unable to practice. Their minds are filled with thoughts of misery and a sense of failure.

You should have faith that every method is a good method and that every individual is a good practitioner. After all, if you are not a good practitioner, why are you still here after five days?

Retreat Three

May 24, 1985 – May 31, 1985

11
Anxiety

With narrow views and doubts,
Haste will slow you down.

Those who take up the study of Buddhism before their views have expanded are subject to fears and doubts. They doubt the method and whether they can reach their objective. Like those who have narrow views and only see what is in front of their eyes, it is a shallow and limited perspective.

This is a common problem on retreat. Everyone should believe that even if they cannot become enlightened this time, they can do so in the future, either in this lifetime or the next. Do you have faith that your method can lead you to enlightenment? Or do you think that it is just the beginning, that later you will learn more advanced methods? Do you believe that Ch'an practice is reliable? Some people may think: "I just came here to take a look. Later, there will be things to learn in other places."

Over the years I have met many people who lack faith. Because of this they reach a certain point and cannot go any further. They may have a partial faith. They may have confidence in themselves but do not trust the method. Or they have faith in the method but do not entirely trust the teacher. Some people may trust the teacher but doubt what levels can actually be reached with Ch'an. This mixture of faith and doubt prevents them from having a deep experience.

Of course, if there were no sense of doubt in the beginning, you would not be motivated to practice. After practicing diligently, you will gradually resolve the problem of doubt. It all depends on your karmic roots. When those with deep karmic roots come in contact with the teachings of Ch'an, they quickly accept them. But those with shallow roots have obstacles which prevent them from believing in themselves, the method, or the teacher. The first requirement of Ch'an is faith. You should believe that you are the ones with deep karmic roots; otherwise, why would you have come to this Ch'an retreat? Compared to the multitude of people in the world, those who can undergo Ch'an training are very few.

Perhaps you still do not believe in yourself, the method, or what I am talking about. But, beginning now, I hope you will start having faith. It does not matter if you are not enlightened yet. Just like a blind person being guided by someone who sees, a person who is not enlightened can borrow a teacher's guidance and experience. It does not matter if you started out with narrow views, as long as you can emerge from them. When you try to understand or judge matters that are beyond your background and experience, it is natural to have some doubts. Use a mind of faith to cure your doubts. It is very important to give rise to a great faith to achieve results. You should have complete faith in what I am teaching. As to the environment, it does not matter whether this is the ideal place to practice.

But the sooner you want to get results, the longer it will take to get anywhere. Once someone was driving me to an appointment. Since he wanted to get me there as quickly as possible, he decided to take a short cut. Though the road was shorter, it turned out that the traffic was heavier than on the normal route.

Another case was a person who was required to take the English equivalency exam in order to apply for a U.S. visa. She thought of a quick method: Before she actually wrote anything down, she would first skim through the entire test to weed out the answers she did not understand. But by the time she went through this first reading, the time was up and nothing was on the answer sheet.

It is the same with practice. If you keep asking yourself, "When am I going to get enlightened?" you will always be in that state of mind and never get anywhere. It is the same when you have trouble getting to sleep and you look at the other people sleeping soundly around you. If you become anxious and keep worrying, "Why can't I sleep? Let me sleep!" you will never get to sleep.

The more you want benefits from Ch'an, the further you will be from obtaining them. In fact, you will only increase your vexations. You may be a highly intelligent person who works very hard and has good karmic roots. But if you are anxious to get enlightened, you have created a barrier between yourself and enlightenment. A tree should be watered very gradually as it is growing. Do not be in a hurry to eat the fruit.

Consider the story about an inexperienced farmer who planted a field of rice. After the crop sprouted, he kept going out to look at it and saying, "Why isn't it growing any faster?" Then he thought of an idea to help it grow. He pulled each stalk out a little taller. The next day he said, "I think I'll go out and help them again." But when he surveyed the field, all the shoots had died.

There is a Chinese saying: "You can't dig a well with one scoop." Another one is: "You can't eat a cake in one bite." It is better for the digestion to chew food until very fine before swallowing. It is the same with practice. Don't try to swallow your practice in one gulp; chew it patiently. You have to be careful and meticulous.

Attach to it and you lose the measure;
The mind will enter a deviant path.

When you grasp onto something, find a happy medium. For example, if you grasp the incense board too tightly, you will hurt the person you are hitting, and may even break the board. But if you hold it too loosely, you cannot aim accurately. You have to hold it just right — not too tight, not too loose. In any activity, you have to find just the right way to do it. This is difficult to accomplish without practice.

I constantly tell people on retreat to relax — mentally and physically. But some people do not know how to do this. Others are too relaxed. As soon as they sit down, they slump over. You cannot practice this way.

Even though your mind is relaxed, you should hold tightly onto the method. Stick to the method and do not let it go. But sometimes people take this advice and become nervous and tense. For instance, in counting the breath, some may become so intent on holding to the method that they end up holding onto the breath itself, thus breathing unnaturally. Or they try to get rid of stray thoughts by counting and breathing faster and faster. This tenses the body. You should hold tight to the method, but at the same time you should not let yourself get tense. To illustrate this, suppose you are walking along a road and it starts bearing to the right. If you keep to a one-track frame of mind of just sticking to the present thought, you will not allow for the bend in the road and walk straight ahead into a tree.

Once I gave someone the hua-t'ou "What is *wu*?" I told her to keep her mind on this one thought, moment to moment, to never leave this question. After a while, her mind jumped to something else, and it became, "I am *wu.*" Rather than correcting herself, she thought, "Shih-fu told me to stay on the present thought." She kept repeating the statement, "I am *wu.*" Finally, she said to me, "There's really no point in this. I already know the answer. There is nothing." (The literal meaning of *wu* is "nothingness.")

When I tell you to hold onto the method, it does not mean to grasp it blindly. Sometimes you have to adjust. I am teaching one method but everyone is unique. Their background, physique, age, experience, are all different. If you just take what I say literally, it could be that you heard it wrong, or that you start practicing it wrong. Therefore, you cannot go by that entirely. You have to test it out by experience. You must be aware of what is going on. If your breath is not flowing smoothly, that should be a signal that

you are not practicing correctly. Ask me about it. There
was a student who was sitting in the "correct" posture,
but his backside became very painful. He was putting too
much pressure on his tailbone. I advised him to lean
slightly forward and straighten his back so that this bone
would not touch the cushion. If you come across a problem like this, you should not continue on in pain because
you think that you are doing as I instructed. Of course
I would not teach you something that causes you pain.
You just sometimes have to make your own adjustments.

12
Being Natural

Let it go and be spontaneous,
Experience no going or staying.
Accord with your nature, unite with the Way,
Wander at ease, without vexation.

The most important thing in practice is to be natural and spontaneous. Being natural does not mean neglecting everything. It requires careful attention. In meditation, you should sit in a natural posture and use your mind in a natural way. Sitting in a natural posture means sitting just right. If you are comfortable when you first assume the sitting posture, even if pains develop in your legs later on, that is still natural. It is unnatural, however, to sit bent over or leaning to one side, or with your head tipped back. A natural posture should follow the demands of your physiology. It is not natural to tighten your stomach muscles or to straighten your back by protruding your chest.

To use your mind in a natural way means to avoid trying to control it. The more you try to control your mind, the more stray thoughts will come up to bother you. In fact, the very fear of stray thoughts is another stray thought. Therefore, if you have many stray thoughts, consider it a natural phenomenon and do not despise them. But on the other hand, if you completely give in to a train of wandering thoughts, that is not correct either. What is the best approach? Pay close attention to the method. If you do that, stray thoughts will be kept to a minimum. It is not that they will not arise, but you will not worry about them. If you are really paying attention to the method, you will be aware of a stray thought as soon as it arises. When it comes up, just let it go. Do not be afraid that another thought may follow it. That fear is an extra stray thought. It is just like a person who is carrying a stack of bowls. If someone says to him, "Be careful! You're going to drop them!" he will drop them. But if nobody says anything, he will just keep going.

Do not fear failure. Whatever happened in the past is past; do not worry about it happening again. Before you meet with success, failure is natural and necessary. As a baby learns to walk, it keeps falling down. Is this failure? Throughout our life we go through similar processes: going to school, pursuing a career, practicing Ch'an. After my first book, someone said to me, "Now you're a success." I said, "No. That book was a failure. I would write it much better if I had to do it again." It is the same with practice; there is never a successful conclusion. When you are working hard, failure is natural. If you have never failed, you have never tried.

On the other hand, you should not have a defeatist attitude, thinking: "As long as I'm going to fail, let me fail."

According to Buddhism, nothing can be a perfect, unqualified success. If you are elected president of the United States, would that be a success? Later on, you would most likely be criticized as a failure. Even President Lincoln would probably consider himself a failure. This is natural. It is when you do not feel successful that you put in the effort. When you no longer need to make an effort, that is true success, or liberation. At that point, there are no more vexations. Nevertheless, you have neither thrown away vexations nor grasped liberation. If you want to hold on to enlightenment and keep away vexations, that is not the true natural state.

But to follow your own nature, in this sense, is not the same as following your personal habits or whims, as in the expression "be natural." Nature here refers to your self-nature, or Buddha nature. Some people think that one can become a Buddha through meditation. This is wrong. The potential for Buddhahood is already within your own nature. If it were true that Buddhahood depended on meditation, then if you stopped meditating after becoming a Buddha, you would become a common person again. The objective of practice is to be in accord with the natural way, so that your true nature can manifest itself. Just practice according to the methods taught by the Buddha and do not worry about being a success. The *Heart Sutra* says, "There is no wisdom and no attainment." Although practice may be trying, even physically painful, if your heart is carefree, nothing will bother you. A carefree approach does not mean not caring about how you practice; it means considering anything that happens as natural. There may be some pain, but there will be no suffering. There is nothing in your mind that you cannot put down.

Bound by thoughts, you depart from the real;
And sinking into a stupor is as bad.

To be in bondage to your thoughts means to be influenced and carried away by various conditions in your surroundings. If you do this, you are grasping the false. You can try to limit your thoughts by using the method. But in fact, as long as the method is still in your mind, you are still abiding in the false, not in the real. But in that case, should you discard the method? The problem with discarding the method is that, while you may seem to have no thoughts, you may still fall into a foggy state. Even though the method is not real, it is even worse to be suspended in a nebulous frame of mind. The ideal state would be to drop the fogginess along with the method, to be unattached to conditions. What does it mean to be unattached to conditions? It means that there are no thoughts in your mind, but whatever appears is perfectly clear.

When you reach this state you will perceive everything as equal. This is because at that time, to you, nothing really exists. Reality cannot be divided into individual people and objects. When nothing is in front of you, it is the same as when there are many things there. In a room full of people, you would not feel crowded and, if the room were empty, you would not feel lonely. Though there is no discrimination in your mind, when relating to people, you distinguish between a monk and a lay person, or a man and a woman. You follow worldly conventions.

However, if your mind is blank, this does not mean you have discarded conditions and reached the state of no thoughts. The blank state would be equivalent to the foggy state, rather than to the truly empty state. Sometimes when you are exhausted, your mind takes a rest and you are not thinking of anything in particular. Do not confuse this with enlightenment.

The method is another way of grasping onto thoughts, but it is a way that allows us to eventually overcome grasping. Using the method effectively is like knitting a sweater. You cannot drop one stitch, otherwise the whole piece will start unravelling. The method should be practiced in the same dense manner. "Dense" means that your attention is so continuous that there is no space in between for any interruptions.

13
Accepting All Realms

It is not good to weary the spirit.
Why alternate between aversion and affection?
If you wish to enter the one vehicle,
Do not be repelled by the sense realm.

Let's return to the opening lines of the poem, "The Supreme Way is not difficult if only you do not pick and choose." Actually, it is not hard to reach enlightenment if you do not grasp or reject. The poem encourages us to practice without attachment. As soon as you become attached to something, you lose the direction of the method.

Yesterday someone asked, "If attaining Buddhahood does not depend on practice, why must I practice?" From the time of Sakyamuni Buddha it was said that Buddhahood cannot be created by practice. This was especially emphasized by the Sixth Patriarch, Hui-Neng. However, practice will help you to discover the innate Buddha nature. Generally, people think of vexations as something inside that have to be destroyed. They think of the Buddha mind as something outside, beyond their reach, that has to be grasped. The constant effort to destroy vexations and grasp the Buddha mind is very burdensome.

Chinese Buddhists have an expression: "In life you don't practice yet on your death bed you would seize the Buddha's foot." In other words, at the last minute, such people are afraid they may drop down into the hells and thus implore the Buddha to take them up to the Pure Land.[1] Their attitude shows that they consider the hells and the Pure Land to be external realms. In reality, all realms lie within ourselves. But it is precisely the greed of someone who wants the Buddha to save him that prevents him from being reborn in the Pure Land. This is because whatever you grasp is false. If you were to succeed in grabbing the Buddha's foot and being transported to the Pure Land, it would turn out to be illusory. The true Pure Land is not located in any particular place and the true Buddha is formless. A Buddha with a form is just a single manifestation of Buddha, a transformation body. Thus you should not be greedy and seek enlightenment without, or be disgusted with vexations within. If you neither desire nor reject anything, you will feel at ease and joyful.

The one vehicle is the Buddha Way. What is the difference between Buddhahood and enlightenment? Buddhahood is attaining the ultimate, whereas enlightenment is seeing Buddha nature without encompassing it fully. You know the taste of the ocean but you have not yet become the ocean.

If you want to follow the Buddha Way, do not be "repelled by the sense realm," or feel any aversion towards your environment. Here at the Center we are bombarded with disturbances — traffic, radios, trains, even the birds and the wind. At first, it is difficult to remain impassive to these noises, but after three days or so you probably do not even hear the cars passing by.

Years ago I had a student who decided on her own to do a solitary retreat. She went to a bungalow colony in the country. At first, she picked the cabin closest to the road, thinking it would be more convenient for shopping. But finding the noise of the traffic too annoying, she kept switching to cabins farther back towards the wooded area. Finally, she got one right in the middle of the woods, only to discover that the sound of the birds was deafening. Later, she asked me, "How did you manage to practice in the mountains?" I told her, "The birds bothered me too, so I stuffed up my ears. But then I noticed the sound of my own heartbeat. The best way is to forget everything around you. That's why you use a method."

Before sitting, you should mentally prepare yourself not to be disturbed by anything that may happen around you. You should have the attitude that even if the house were burning, you would not get up from your seat. Someone usually asks, "But what if your house really does catch on fire?" I say, "If you are worried now that your house may someday catch on fire, you certainly won't sit successfully."

This also includes not being disturbed by the person sitting next to you. On one winter retreat a student wrapped herself in a blanket while sitting. Every time she sat to meditate, she swung the blanket around her body, accidentally striking her neighbor in the face. For three days he was annoyed by it. But he remembered that I had said one should not be influenced by other people. He then

cultivated an attitude that whenever she struck him with
her blanket it just meant that she was preparing to meditate; it had nothing to do with him.

(1) Pure Land: The Western Paradise of Amitabha Buddha,
one of many blissful realms in the Mahayana, each associated
with a specific Buddha. The main requirement for entering
the Pure Land after death is the wholehearted expression of
faith in the compassion of Amitabha Buddha. Belief in the
Pure Land gave rise to the Pure Land School, whose primary
method of practice is to recite Amitabha Buddha's name.

14
Limiting the Environment

With no aversion to the sense realm,
You become one with true enlightenment.

The true practitioner is not affected by the environment. If you enjoy your surroundings too much, you will not even think about practicing. But if you despise your surroundings, you will not be able to practice even if you try.

It is impossible to throw off your environment all at once. It must be peeled away like an onion. In order to do this, it would be helpful to think of the environment as three concentric circles. The outermost circle is the world around you, the middle one is your body, and the inner circle is your mind. On the first day of retreat, I said that you must forget your affairs in the world outside of the Ch'an Center; in other words, put aside all thoughts of past and future. But once you do that, new thoughts related to the world inside the Center will come up. It may be a smaller world, but it is still external to the body. You may be distracted by the others, or you may become attached to my words, or even to my presence. Some people take notice of where I am in the room, and anticipate what I am going to do next.

If you limit your attention to your body, either you feel comfortable or uncomfortable. It is difficult to totally forget the body. Your legs are painful, your back hurts, your head aches, your neck is strained, your skin itches, or you just feel tired. Ignore any sensations, pleasant or unpleasant, that may arise. On the other hand, if the pain is too great to ignore, consider your body as a corpse. To be able to conquer your pain and your fear of death requires great determination. If you can develop this will power in Ch'an training, you will be able to succeed in any other endeavor.

Once you narrow yourself down to the mental environment, there are two things you are involved with — the method, and stray thoughts. You will find that your mind is just as full as the outside environment. As the *Sutra of Complete Enlightenment* says, "Mental activities are just a shadow of the sensory world." Thus if you manage to dispense with all your environments, you will attain the state of no mind, and you will reach a great realization.

The wise have no motives;
Fools put themselves in bondage.

The more you strive after liberation, the more you tie yourself up. This is also true of seeking safety, health and security. Once I was approached by a life insurance agent who did not know I was a monk. He said, "Our insurance policy is excellent. No matter what happens to you, your wife and children will be taken care of." I asked, "What if I don't have a wife and children?" He had nothing to say after that. He saw that I had no worries about death.

One monk I know actually took out a policy. I asked him, "Why did you do that?" He said, "So that after I die there will be money for my funeral rites and burial." I said, "Don't you think that a monk would be buried in any case? Even if he is not, maggots would eventually dispose of the body."

A practitioner should not consider his own security. Otherwise, he would not be able to practice in the mountains far away from society. Whatever fears or desires you can discard will give you that much more freedom. But whatever protection you seek will become your karmic obstruction.

This is why you should not look for something here to take home with you. On the contrary, you should try to lose what you brought in. Why should you add to your burdens? After you learn something and absorb it, then it becomes part of you. Just as when you eat, you obtain the nutrients from the food and then eliminate the waste. If you retained everything, then your health would be in serious trouble.

15
One Dharma

One dharma is not different from another.
The deluded mind clings to whatever it desires.

In complete enlightenment, there are no different dharmas, or objects of existence; there is only the one Dharma. But you cannot say that this one, perfect Dharma either exists or does not exist. To exist, it would have to be opposed to something else that does not, and vice versa. Buddhism does not speak in terms of opposites or of the absolute. Nothing can be absolutely affirmed or denied. When you attach to or reject anything, you are in a position of duality with that object.

In most religions, if you reach a stage where you identify completely with the universe, it would be considered the ultimate, or great harmony. But, according to Buddha Dharma, this is not the highest stage, since some thought still remains. After you concentrate your scattered mind, you reach the stage of unified mind. There are various levels of unified mind — the unity of self and universe, the unity of body and mind, and beyond this, just one mind remaining. The unity of self and universe is a joyous experience. You feel at one with the flowers and the trees and with everyone around you. You may feel liberated. But this is still not Ch'an.

If there is only one Dharma, it is erroneous to seek the Dharma outside or within yourself. That would create a duality. Some people imagine that getting enlightened is seeing a Buddha nature within themselves. I tell you that there is nothing to see. Whatever you see is an illusion. Buddha nature is empty nature. If you seek something, how can you get to emptiness? The *Diamond Sutra* says that there is no Dharma form and also that there is nothing that is not the form of the Dharma. Thus we should not become attached to either existence or emptiness.

> *Using mind to cultivate mind —*
> *Is this not a great mistake?*

When you practice, you are using your mind to work on your mind. You use a deluded thought, the method, to reduce your other deluded thoughts. But the real Ch'an is methodless. No-method is to practice with nothing in your mind, and to be clearly aware that there is nothing in your mind. Moment by moment, maintain the state of no-thought. If a thought arises, just return to no-thought. If I ask you a question while you were in this state you would answer spontaneously. If you have to think about what to say, your mind is already moving. Nowadays, it is impossible for most to maintain this state of mind. In the past, practitioners were able to put in twenty or more years of solid practice. It is difficult for one with a daily work routine to do this. But you should still be aware that although you rely on a method, whether it be breath counting, kung-an, or reciting the Buddha's name, it is not the true Ch'an. The true Ch'an transcends all methods.

> *The erring mind begets tranquility and confusion;*
> *In enlightenment there are no likes or dislikes.*

Before enlightenment, people distinguish between a quiescent state, which they call "nirvana," and a chaotic state, which they call "samsara." They want to leave samsara behind and enter nirvana. But seeking to leave the world of noise and confusion to get to a peaceful place is like looking for a rabbit with horns. There is no Buddha Dharma to be found outside of this world. In the *Platform Sutra*, the Sixth Patriarch says that to leave the world is to be in the world. The true practitioner does not despise a chaotic environment, nor does he need to go deep into the mountains. He just flows with causes and conditions. Wherever he is, that is his place of practice. He does not feel cramped in a crowded place, nor does he feel lonely in an isolated place.

Retreat Four

June 28, 1985 – July 3, 1985

16
The Dreaming Mind

The duality of all things
Issues from false discriminations.

Some examples of dualities, or opposites, are: you and me, the Buddha and sentient beings, nirvana and samsara, wisdom and ignorance. In the *Platform Sutra*, the Sixth Patriarch enumerates thirty-six pairs of opposites. One who seeks wisdom and rejects ignorance as if they were opposites is deluded. A person who thinks of himself as wise is full of self-pride. On the other hand, a person who thinks of himself as ignorant is full of self-pity.

The *Heart Sutra* says: "There is no wisdom and no attainment; with nothing to attain, *bodhisattvas*,[1] relying on *prajnaparamita*,[2] have no obstructions in their minds." This is why you should come to retreat — not to attain anything, but to practice. Some people approach retreat as if they were a caterpillar hoping to transform themselves into a beautiful butterfly. This kind of motivation is an obstacle to practice.

During retreat I use various means to inspire you to practice, including harsh language. To take this to heart and consider yourself a worthless, incapable person, or else to fight back and deny what I say are both incorrect attitudes. My aim is to whittle down your self-pride or self-pity. However harshly I may seem to treat you, do not dwell on it and feel sorry for yourself. Nor should you feel happy if I praise you. However, from my point of view, I have to discern between the types of practitioners. Some do not react well under pressure. They are like tender bean sprouts that have to be treated gently. Others, whose practice has matured somewhat, can handle more forceful techniques; the more they are pressured, the better they do.

A dream, an illusion, a flower in the sky —
How could they be worth grasping?

From the age of ten, I have always seen flower-like images in the sky. This is due to a malfunction of my eyesight. But I have learned not to pay any attention to them. Whatever you consider to be solid or real are only flowers in the sky. Even genuine achievements are still false in the sense that they are not permanent. There was an aerospace company that advertised an innovative way to continue on after death. They would shoot a satellite containing your ashes into orbit around the earth, and there it would spin for about 36,000 years. Even though this seems like an eternity, about nine times the length of civilized history, the time will eventually pass. The earth itself will disappear. There is no sense in trying to pretend otherwise.

From the time we were born, up to the present moment, not much time has elapsed. Not too long from now, we will die. Nothing much has really transpired in that period of time. Faced with this situation, and seeing how temporary everything is, we are impelled to seek something permanent and real. But there is nothing like that to be found.

People sometimes ask Ch'an masters, "What happened to you? What did you realize?" And the master will often give a cryptic reply, such as "Cows eating grass," or "I wonder where this clothing was made." Why don't they just say something like: "I had a great enlightenment experience! I really did! Now I understand what the Buddha is all about."? They do not answer this way because the idea of a special, incomparable enlightenment is an illusion, and they know that. At a retreat once a student had a small experience, and later I asked him, "How do you feel now?" He said, "Ah! The rice is really tasty."

But if nothing is real or lasting, what is the point of coming to retreat and practicing Ch'an? The point is that during the course of practice, you may come to realize that everything around you, as well as whatever you seek out of life, are illusory. The ordinary person does not know this. Even if you convince yourself intellectually that everything is illusory, you may still have a lurking concept of the reality of things and be attached to them. To be able to actually treat them as transient is another thing entirely.

Gain and loss, right and wrong —
Discard them all at once.

Some of you had pleasant experiences today, and others just ended up with aching legs. If you spend your time hoping that a pleasant experience will return, or trying to avoid pain, you will become more aware of the passing of time. You will feel restless and think, "Today has gone by already and I've wasted my time." Some people have this attitude when, after a day or two, they feel they have not made any progress. They tell themselves that they could be doing so many other things at home, or furthering their career. If you feel you have not gotten anywhere, discard this attitude immediately. If you continue to dwell on these things, you probably will give up and go home.

> *If the eyes do not close in sleep,*
> *All dreams will cease of themselves.*

"The eyes" are your awareness. The instant you lose awareness of just what you are doing at the moment, you are dreaming. Dreaming means being carried away by your wandering thoughts and unable to stop them. As in actual dreams, these wandering thoughts are either connected with the past, or anticipate the future. They are not concerned with the present, because the present is just keeping your mind on your method.

People often concentrate intensely on the method for a short time and then say, "Well, I'll take a break now. I'll just put the method aside and let my mind wander a little bit." This is a wrong way to practice. Using the method can be likened to pumping air into a tire. The minute you stop pumping, the air starts to leak and the tire will eventually go flat. You may think that by putting down the method and relaxing for a while, you are re-charging your energy. In fact what you are really doing is letting the air out of your tires.

This is common among beginners. They often make the mistake of exerting physical energy to fight against wandering thoughts. As a result their bodies become tense and the blood rushes to their heads, and after a time they feel a need to relax. But those who know how to work well summon up their concentration in a clear, relaxed manner. They do not belabor themselves with an excess of physical energy or struggle with their method. Instead, they maintain a natural moment-to-moment awareness.

This lucid awareness should not only be practiced while sitting, but also when you are eating and working. Let everything else drop away and concern yourself only with the method. If you can do this uninterruptedly for a period of time, I guarantee that all of your dreams will disappear, including your method. But in fact your mind is totally on the method then.

It is common for people to want a vacation after working hard. But during the vacation, their minds will scatter and their concentration will dissipate. If you alternate work and vacation in this way, you will never get beyond a certain level of practice. By practicing daily meditation and going on retreats, at least you are pumping the air into the tire to some extent. But you should be aware that this kind of interrupted practice is not the ideal approach to Ch'an.

(1) *bodhisattva*: (Sanskrit, "awakened being"). In Mahayana Buddhism, an enlightened person on the path to Buddha-hood, who renounces entry into nirvana until all sentient beings are saved. Contrasted to an *arhat*, who passes into nirvana after complete enlightenment.

(2) *prajnaparamita*: (Sanskrit, "perfection of wisdom"). One of the ten *paramitas*, or perfections, i.e., virtues practiced by *bodhisattvas*; refers to the perfection of the virtue of wisdom (*prajna*).

17
Climbing the Crystal Mountain

If the mind does not discriminate,
All dharmas are of one suchness.
The essence of one suchness is profound;
Unmoving, conditioned things are forgotten.

When you do not discriminate, you see everything as one. There is no difference between mind and body, inside and outside. Your mind is unified. You have left behind the sense of small self and have entered the state of great self. You are imbued with tremendous confidence. If you want to call this oneness "enlightenment," there is nothing wrong with that, but it is not Ch'an enlightenment. To experience Ch'an, you must probe the mysterious essence of suchness.

I have emphasized that when there is a sense of one, there are actually two. To go a step further, when you sense that even one does not exist, this is the experience of *wu*, or emptiness. But because you have a concept of emptiness, your mind is still subtly present. Ultimately, even *wu* does not exist. Emptiness is still within the three realms of existence, but this is already more advanced than just non-discrimination.

Ch'an is a lively practice which does not neglect the world. The Sixth Patriarch said, "Samadhi is not Ch'an." Practitioners of Ch'an lead normal lives. They do not speak of oneness or emptiness. The only difference is that there is no obstruction or attachment in their minds.

Contemplate all dharmas as equal,
And you return to things as they are.

In fact, these two lines refer to different things. "Contemplate all dharmas as equal" refers to non-discrimination, or one mind. "Things as they are" refers to returning to the ordinary life. In the state of one mind, the small self has died, but the great self is still present. There has to be a great death before we can experience a great rebirth. With this great rebirth will come a great love. When the great self dies, we enter no-self, or Ch'an.

Once a student misunderstood this talk about small death and great death. He asked me to let him die here on retreat. In this way, he would accumulate merit in the company of his fellow practitioners. I told him, "If you die here you would only go to hell. It's a very hot time of year, and if we keep your corpse lying around, the smell will interfere with others' practice." The death I am talking about is not a physical death. It is the death of your self-centered mind. This cannot come about merely by wishing to die. If you killed yourself a thousand times it would not do you any good. You would still be in samsara.

When the subject disappears,
There can be no measuring or comparing.

If you let go of every thought object, there will be nothing
to distinguish yourself from, and you will disappear. Today
someone remarked, "I still have a self left. I have to get
rid of this self." I said, "Self is not something you can get
rid of. Self is not inside; it is not identical to your body
or your mind. Rather, self is precisely the object of all of
your thoughts and actions. Other than this, there is no
self." Can your mind have no object? Usually we think
of the method as something we can rely on, as a bridge
to get us across the river. But Ch'an is really the method
of no-method. There is no bridge provided, because there
is no river. If you let go of your attaching mind, at that
very moment you are enlightened.

Practice is a foolish endeavor, like climbing a crystal
mountain covered with oil. As you try to climb, you
constantly slip back down. Nevertheless, you have no
choice. You must continue climbing. You climb until you
are completely exhausted, and suddenly you find yourself
on the top of the mountain. But you realize you are still
at the original spot. If you have not covered any distance
at all, why was it necessary to climb the mountain? The
answer is that before you started climbing you did not
realize that you were already on the top of the mountain.
Only a fool would try to climb a slippery crystal mountain.
If you are intelligent, you should go home right now.
However, if you are willing to recognize being a fool, then
take the time to climb the mountain.

18
Rest and Activity

Stop activity and there is no activity;
When activity stops, there is no rest.
Since two cannot be established,
How can there be one?

In Ch'an practice it is not necessary to stop wandering thoughts. The reason is that activity and rest are not in opposition. But if there is no such duality, then there is no oneness to speak of either.

We call this retreat a Ch'an retreat but actually it is just a suffering or training retreat. Ch'an is methodless, but everyone here is using certain methods. The purpose of the methods is to replace your wandering thoughts. But the methods themselves are wandering thoughts. Therefore, to use a method to stop the activity of your thoughts is in itself activity. There can be no such thing as rest.

Let us talk about rest. In samadhi, the mind moves so slowly it feels as if it were at rest. But this rest is only relative. Even if you get to the highest level of samadhi, the so-called "neither thinking nor not thinking samadhi," your mind is still moving in a subtle way. However, most people would understand this to be rest.

On the other hand, it is possible for the mind to seem to be at rest even when it is moving fast. To illustrate, one can copy a two-hour taped lecture onto another tape in the space of one minute. But if you listen to this lecture as it is being copied, you would not be able to distinguish the various words. You would hear only a single sound.

Likewise, a person with an agile mind can resolve many problems without effort. He would not be conscious of any strenuous mental activity. A person with slower mental faculties, however, may sense more vexations and feel that his mind has gone through a lot of thinking, when actually it has dealt with fewer problems.

In the very ultimate,
Rules and standards do not exist.

The ultimate is beyond all human rules and laws. It cannot be judged by worldly standards. Thoroughly enlightened people spontaneously help sentient beings in accordance with causes and conditions. Their actions are not bound by the moral codes of society. This is not the case for ordinary people. We must abide by certain principles and rules. But if the thoroughly enlightened are bound by these laws, it would not be genuine liberation. For them there is no boundary between activity and rest.

But the misinterpretation of this truth has caused great harm. Some people think that Ch'an advertises moral indifference, that Ch'an practitioners in general are free to ignore ethical principles. There are some who admit they are not enlightened, but nevertheless refuse to recognize accepted rules of behavior. They reason that if they imitate the ways of an enlightened person, they will gradually pick up the enlightened spirit.

Master Hsu-Yun, though a monk, never shaved his head. Thus, he appeared to be one of those who did not observe the rules. However, he insisted that his disciples have shaved heads. The reason why Hsu-Yun never shaved is that during his long period of practice, he did not have the time. Later, when he was an accomplished master he was already accustomed to not shaving. Though his hair was unruly, he conducted his life was very rigorously and in strict accord with the precepts. A Ch'an master may seem carefree, but behind superficial appearances there is a solid foundation. It is only upon a solid foundation that one can draw on a truly liberated spirit not limited by rules.

> *Develop a mind of equanimity,*
> *And all deeds are put to rest.*

A mind of equanimity is a mind without distinctions; in other words, there is no rest and no activity. When your mind is in this condition, whatever you do is the same as not doing anything at all. Your mind is at rest within activity. There is a saying that on becoming an *arhat*,[1] whatever has to be done has already been accomplished. Similarly, in the *Platform Sutra*, it is said that when there is no concern about good or evil, you can stretch out your legs and take a nap. When the mind is not making distinctions, there is no self, no other, no good, no bad. There is really nothing that needs to be done. This does not mean that you do nothing, but that your mind is in a state of rest. In fact, it is not even correct to speak of *your* mind. A person in this condition uses the mind of sentient beings.

> *Anxious doubts are completely cleared.*
> *Right faith is made upright.*

With a mind of equanimity, there is no longer any confusion or doubt about the Dharma. Even if you believe in the Dharma, but have not experienced realization, that is not called "right faith." You must have your own realization so that your faith will be affirmed and never change. Your mind will be straightforward without distortion. This means that whatever you endeavor, you will not make the wrong decision from the point of view of Dharma. The ordinary person may make erroneous judgments and actions, because he uses a mind of distinctions.

(1) *arhat*: (Sanskrit, "worthy one"). Practitioner, especially in the Hinayana (Theravadin) tradition, who has extinguished all attachments and defilements, and stands on the threshold of nirvana. Contrasted to a bodhisattva of the Mahayana tradition, who foregoes the promise of nirvana until all sentient beings are delivered.

19
Leaving No Trace

Nothing lingers behind,
Nothing can be remembered.
Bright and empty, functioning naturally,
The mind does not exert itself.

After a bird has flown from one tree to another, what trace did it leave in the air? Again, when you stand in front of a mirror, you see your image reflected in it. But after you have gone, what is left in the mirror? Your mind should be like this; any event that occurs should leave no trace in your mind. We cannot deny that the bird has actually flown a certain distance, or that the mirror has reflected you. But it is precisely because the bird did not leave a trace that other birds are free to fly over the same route, and it is precisely because the mirror does not retain your image that other people can also see their images. If traces were left in the sky, would it look as spacious as it does to us now? If the mirror retained images, would it still be able to reflect?

Likewise, the accumulation of knowledge and experiences only adds obstructions. For instance, whatever you have learned previously from other teachers is like the trace of a bird, or the image left behind on a mirror. If these things stay in your mind on retreat, you will not be able to absorb my teachings because there will be an overlap of images. On the first evening I told you to forget everything that happened in the past; do not attempt to compare what happens on this retreat with your former experiences.

Not remembering anything does not mean that you are like a stone or a piece of wood. Your mind is still clearly aware of knowing certain things but does not try to bring up these memories as criteria for comparing and judging. The bird did fly from tree to tree, and the mirror did reflect people, but they have nothing to do with you. Phenomena may change, but your mind is not moved by them.

Today someone found the Ch'an hall too hot, and so kept taking off layers of clothing; but when he looked around, it seemed that everyone else did not mind the heat. Finally he could bear it no longer and came to talk to me. I told him that he felt so hot because he was thinking that it was hot. If his mind was on practice he would not be aware of the heat. He took my advice and it worked. It is the mind that generates these vexations. The environment may contribute, but if your mind does not cooperate, it will not pose a problem for you.

> *It is not a place of thinking,*
> *Difficult for reason and emotion to fathom.*

It is impossible to explain the state when there is nothing left in the mind. For the past few evenings, I have been talking about no mind. A few people have asked me, "What is this no mind you are talking about?" I said, "No mind is just no mind. Even if I were to tell you, you still would not know. You cannot use your reasoning or knowledge to imagine it. You can only know by personal experience."

When I was in my teens someone told me he had a ringing in his ears. I asked him to describe it, and he explained it was like the humming of bees. I still did not understand what it felt like. Later when I was forty, I experienced it myself. If physiological experiences are difficult to imagine, all the more so with Ch'an, which is beyond all normal experience.

In the Dharma Realm of true suchness,
There is no other, no self.

True suchness refers to things as they really are, without eternal existence. Some think that true suchness is something eternal that can be held on to, but actually there is no such thing. Neither is there any Dharma Realm. True suchness is neither self nor other. Many practitioners seek to discover their self-nature, which they identify with Buddha nature, or true suchness. But this implies a certain existence. True suchness is neither yourself nor another.

Someone said to me, "I know that the self I am familiar with is an illusion. I want to find the true one." I replied, "The self you have now is illusory. But even the true self is illusory. Nevertheless, you must try to find it. If you don't find it, you won't know it is an illusion."

To accord with it is vitally important;
Only refer to "not-two."

In not-two all things are in unity;
Nothing is excluded.

To be in accord with true suchness, two things cannot be different; they are "not-two" in the sense of not being more than one. However, it would not be meaningful to speak of something according with itself. Thus, we cannot speak of one or two. We can only say "not-two." In true suchness, there is accordance with all sentient beings. The Buddha is in accord with sentient beings, and sentient beings can be in accord with each other. Accordance is a communication, or connection, between two things, such that they form a unity. For example, in marriage, two people come together without losing their own individuality.

In not-two everything is included. In fact, "not-two" refers to no mind, the mind of *bodhi*.[1] If you say something is there, you would be wrong. If you say nothing is there, you would also be wrong. Therefore, existence and non-existence are not-two. If this is the case, everything is included. The *Platform Sutra* states that vexation is the same as *bodhi*. Those who do not practice Ch'an are not aware of their deepest vexations. When you discover the extent of your vexations and think that you are not making any progress, then you are really practicing. Only when you realize your problems is it possible to resolve them.

(1) *bodhi*: (Sanskrit, "awakened"). State of enlightened mind, characterized by having experienced one's own Buddha nature.

20
True Suchness

The wise throughout the ten directions
All enter this principle.
This principle is neither hurried nor slow —
One thought for ten thousand years.

The word translated here as "wise" has multiple meanings. In Sanskrit, the word *prajna* can be used in the sense of worldly wisdom, or it can be used in the sense of wisdom transcending the world. Finally, it can be simultaneously worldly and transcendent. This is the highest *prajna* referred to in Mahayana Buddhism. To determine which sense of *prajna* is being used, you have to look at the context. Here, "wise" refers to the highest *prajna*. All beings with *prajna* will have to enter through the same door. *Tsung*, translated as "principle" here, can also be taken to mean the Dharma Realm of true suchness that I spoke of yesterday.

This principle is neither long nor short in a temporal sense. If you say that it is long, or lasting, you are falling into the "view of constancy." Buddha Dharma does not accept the view that there is something eternal and unchanging. On the other hand, if you say that it is short, then you are prone to the "view of termination." In Buddha Dharma both constancy and termination are considered extreme, or "outer path" views. But Ch'an often speaks of that which is "beginningless" and "endless." Does this contradict the Buddhist view of nothing being eternal? You should understand that even though everything is in a constant flux, the principle of change itself does go on indefinitely. Thus to say that this principle is not eternal would also be incorrect.

There are two possible interpretations of the line "One thought for ten thousand years." One is that the mind simply does not move. But is this possible? Even in deep levels of samadhi, as long as it is a worldly samadhi, the mind is still moving in a subtle way. In fact, as you get into ever deeper levels, you may be aware of the movement of your mind in the previous level, even if you are not aware of the movement at the present level. You realize that what you took to be a still mind, actually consisted of many minute fluctuations. Therefore, this interpretation does not hold here.

The second explanation is that there is no mind. "Ten thousand years" is a term used to indicate unlimited time. No mind is unlimited; one instant can encompass ten thousand years.

Abiding nowhere yet everywhere,
The ten directions are right before you.

This single incense board is true suchness in its entirety. But if you think that only the incense board is true suchness, you are wrong. True suchness is everywhere; nothing is separate from true suchness. The previous two lines referred to Ch'an as being unlimited by time. These two lines are speaking of the limitlessness of space. If you can grasp a small spot, you have access to totality. At the tip of a fine strand of hair all the Buddhas of the three times and the ten directions are turning the Dharma wheel. If a person who is thoroughly enlightened reads these lines, he would say, "Indeed it is just like that! It is not anything different." But for someone with only a theoretical understanding, it is like gazing at flowers through a mist, obscured by your own thoughts.

> *The smallest is the same as the largest*
> *In the realm where delusion is cut off.*
> *The largest is the same as the smallest;*
> *No boundaries are visible.*

In the state where the spot in front of your eyes is equivalent to totality, there is no room for illusory dharmas. Illusory dharmas are the dharmas of distinctions, of small and large, of positing one thing against another. Usually, we see something as small because it is in relation to something bigger than itself. To say that the largest is equivalent to the smallest erases all boundaries. This refers again to true suchness.

Someone asked, "After a person attains Buddhahood, where would he be?" There are three bodies of the Buddha, the *trikaya*[1] — the transformation body, the reward body, and the Dharma body. The transformation body appears in a particular time and place in the human realm. The reward body also appears for the sake of sentient beings; for this reason, it is limited in location. But the Dharma body of the Buddha is not limited to any time or place. You cannot say it is here or it is there. It is simultaneously the largest and the smallest. It has the greatest power, but at the same time it has no power whatsoever. It is smaller than anything we can know of, because it has no self. But because the Dharma body of the Buddha has no self, all sentient beings are identical to this body. Wherever sentient beings need the Buddha, the Dharma body can function for their benefit.

> *Existence is precisely emptiness;*
> *Emptiness is precisely existence.*

The Dharma body of the Buddha, or true suchness, cannot be said to "exist" because there is no self. However, it can be experienced because if your practice reaches a certain depth. True suchness is not identical to nothingness. Everything that exists in the three times and ten directions is never separate from it. "Emptiness" refers to no self and "existence" refers to causes and conditions.

Some Ch'an masters speak only of existence and some speak only of emptiness. Others sometimes speak of existence and sometimes speak of emptiness, depending on the audience. But they are all speaking of the same thing. One time a monk complained to me, "In my opinion, most, if not all, Ch'an masters are lunatics. If you talk to them about existence, they uphold the idea of emptiness.

If you talk to them about emptiness, they affirm existence." Ch'an cannot be spoken or conceived. Indeed, since it cannot be expressed in words, whatever you say about it, as existence or emptiness, can be criticized.

If it is not like this,
Then you must not preserve it.

You have to let go of your previous views: self-attachment, attachment to existence, emptiness, large and small, boundedness, unboundedness, truth and illusion.

One is everything,
Everything is one.

True suchness is identical to all phenomena and all phenomena are never separated from true suchness. It must be understood in this sense, and not in the sense that all phenomena reduce to one. There is no distinction between unification and non-unification in true suchness. Otherwise, taking these two lines literally would imply that if one person becomes a Buddha, everyone else has to become a Buddha. Or, all sentient beings must attain Buddhahood before there can be even one Buddha, since all sentient beings are one. This would not hold on a common sense level, yet it can be understood on the deeper level just explained.

If you can be like this,
Why worry about not finishing?

When you know that true suchness is identical to all phenomena, then there are no worries about getting enlightened or attaining Buddhahood.

Faith and mind are not two;
Non-duality is faith in mind.

If you have faith in the mind of equanimity and non-distinction, you have faith in no mind. However, the mind of the person who has faith is the mind of an ordinary sentient being. What the poem says is that the mind of faith is not separate from no mind, the mind that is the object of the faith. This is the same as saying that true suchness is identical to all phenomena. Although the two minds are identical, you must begin with faith to give you direction in your practice. Not only must you have faith in no mind, but you must have faith in every single word of this poem and act accordingly. In this way, you can attain the mind of no mind.

The path of words is cut off;
There is no past, no future, no present.

During the course of practice, we employ the use of words to guide us. But when faith and mind are not separate, all words and language are unnecessary, including the poem *Faith in Mind*. Again, during practice, there is a distinction between past, present and future. Progress is measured in terms of time, but when faith and mind are not separate, these distinctions are abolished.

Once a monk asked Hsu-Yun, "Is there time in samadhi?" Hsu-Yun answered, "If there is time in samadhi, it is not samadhi." The monk asked, "In that case, can you say there is no time in samadhi?" Hsu-Yun said, "If there is no time in samadhi, where is the person?" In samadhi the mind is holding to one thought, so there is no awareness of time. But the meditator is still in the present moment, not in the past or the future. However, if you go one step further into no mind, you cannot even be in the present. The present can only exist in the mind, in relation to the past and the future.

(1) *trikaya*: (Sanskrit, "threebodies"). Mahayana doctrine of the tripartite bodies of the Buddha: (1) *nirmanakaya*, the transformation body, manifesting as a human being, as in Sakyamuni; (2) *sambhogakaya*, the bliss body of the venerated Buddhas, experienced only by enlightened *bodhisattvas*; (3) *dharmakaya*, the supreme body of all the transcendent Buddhas.